WHY LAWYERS SUCK!

Hacking the Legal System, Part 1

Melody A. Kramer

Legal Greenhouse Publishing

San Diego, California USA

Legal Greenhouse Publishing
a KR Ventures, Inc. company
4010 Sorrento Valley Blvd., Ste. 400
San Diego, CA 92121
Visit our website at www.legalgreenhouse.com

Limits of Liability and Disclaimer of Warranty:
The purpose of this book is to educate and entertain. The authors and/ or publisher do not guarantee that anyone following these techniques, suggestions, tips, ideas, or strategies will become successful in any particular legal matter.

Printed and bound in the United States of America

ISBN: 978-0-615-95216-1

Library of Congress Control Number: 2015918648

Book designed by Stefan Merour
Book cover design by Bella Guzmán

Dedication

To my Uncle Will, who inspired me to love the law,

To Professor John Snowden who gave me
permission to subvert the dominant paradigm, and

To my daughter, Noelle, whose unwavering
support makes me believe anything is possible

Acknowledgements

This book would not have been possible without the help, encouragement, and financial support of so many people. I am grateful beyond words to Stephanie Anderson, Gabriella Coniglio, Heather Hagen, Ted & Cori Kramer, Herb & Betty Kramer, Christopher D. Kwoka, Jack & Nan McCartney, DeAnna McGough, Steinar & Marianne Myhre, Jeanine Sachs, Damon Scaggs, Marcy Shoberg, my Hera Hub family, and dozens of other financial and content contributors.

A special thank you goes to my publishing coaches, the late Jan B. King and Candace George Conradi, who helped me bring my book concept to life, and to Bethany Kelly, who helped me convert my manuscript into an actual book.

How to Use this Book

This book is intended to be an entertaining read, great for passing the time on an airplane flight or for a lazy afternoon curled up in your jammies in front of the fire with a warm mug of hot chocolate in your hands.

However, the book is also filled with helpful "hacks," ways you can use your heightened understanding of what is going on in lawyers' minds to directly benefit your interactions with them. There are ways to reduce legal fees, reduce frustration, and minimize the negative effects of disputes on your business operations and life. These hacks are useful for individual legal matters and massive lawsuits, and everything in between.

In true lawyer fashion, however, I must include this caveat—nothing in this book is intended as a substitute for legal advice for any particular legal matter and no attorney-client relationship is created between me, the author, and you, the reader, here.

We love collecting stories about how the hacks in this book have directly benefitted you in your experience with lawyers. Please send us an email to share your experiences to stories@legalgreenhouse.com.

Contents

PREFACE

*"The greater fool is someone with the perfect
blend of self-delusion and ego to think that he [or she]
can succeed where others have failed.
This whole country was made by greater fools."*

- Aaron Sorkin (from HBO's "*The Newsroom*")

"How many lawyer jokes are there?" I was asked once as a young lawyer. "Millions?" I guessed. "Only three— the rest are true stories." My friend may have been making an attempt at humor, but it fell flat, then and now. It wasn't funny then because I thought she was wrong. It isn't funny now because I know she was right. Lawyers suck! They are dishonest and mean, deceitful and spiteful. The fact that you picked up this book and started reading tells me that you have had the same experience. Despite my efforts to not be *one of those lawyers*, I know I have been, at least on occasion.

"But," you may say, "not every lawyer sucks," and you are right. It doesn't matter, though. Have you ever tried to cover the stench of manure by mixing in a few fragrant wildflowers? It doesn't fix the problem of the stench.

Lawyers suck. So what? Why do I care to point out this obvious fact of the universe? Why write a book about it? I mean, who cares *why* lawyers

1

suck? If you can avoid them, do so, like the plague. If you need one, just suck it up and hope to survive the ordeal. Right? What if you could have a few hacks to help you deal with lawyers, hacks that could save you money and frustration, hacks that could even the playing field just a little bit?

I think I may be writing this book as a sort of penance. I'm confident that I have been hung in effigy more than once by opposing counsel or parties, even an occasional judge, once or twice even a client, and I hereby acknowledge that perhaps, on occasion, I deserved it. Apologies without a sincere effort to make amends, however, are insufficient.

You, the public, have a right to some transparency about the lawyers that affect your lives every day in significant, and sometimes harmful, ways. You have a right to have a little understanding of "why" they act the way they do. I am writing this book because the "why" isn't what you may think and knowing the "why" opens you up to opportunities to reduce legal fees and shorten legal disputes, and will save you a ton of heartache and sleepless nights. As you read through each chapter, you will gain new angles of understanding and practical steps you can take to counteract lawyers' negative attributes.

We have an insane legal and judicial system in this country that needs to be changed, fundamentally and immediately, beginning with acknowledgement of the problems inherent with lawyers themselves. Until wholesale change happens, however, this book will give you some practical solutions—hacks—for dealing with the current legal system.

Despite 20+ brutal years as a trial lawyer, I still have a shred of optimism left. I think it is possible for lawyers and the legal profession to change for the better, if only they had a better understanding of how they became reviled in the first place and their clients had a better understanding of how to deal with them.

In short, I am writing this book because I am a greater fool.

Melody A. Kramer, Esq.

CONSPIRACY OF SILENCE

Nothing makes us so lonely as our secrets.

-Paul Tournier

I n our society of reality TV, smart phones, and surveillance cameras, there are few secrets left. However, what happens in courtrooms, judges' chambers, and behind the closed doors of law firms and deposition rooms, continues to be hidden behind a veil of secrecy and silence.

To be sure, there have been a handful of court cases on live TV in the past few decades, such as the OJ Simpson and Casey Anthony trials. However, the bulk of legal activities and the daily lives of lawyers are never subjected to third-party, objective scrutiny, either in person, or via audio or video recording.

The legal world remains a bastion of secrets and silence, all meticulously protected by laws, rules, and unwritten standards of behavior. If history teaches us nothing else, it should teach us this lesson--behind the walls of secrecy, abuses will occur.

Absence of transparency, inefficiencies, inequities, and abuse go unchecked for decades and centuries. Any mental health professional will tell you that keeping secrets can cause profound emotional trauma and frequently lead to excessive use of alcohol or drugs, or sometimes even to suicide. In fact, the secrecy often can cause more damage than the original trauma.

Secrets lawyers keep are from many sources: client confidences, verbal and psychological abuse among opposing counsel, abusive and bad behavior of judges, sometimes even abusive conduct by clients directed at their lawyers. Disclosure to authorities such as the bar association or court does nothing to fix the problem, and can lead to discipline or loss of license, or jeopardize their client's case.

> If history teaches us nothing else,
> it should teach us this lesson--behind the
> walls of secrecy, abuses will occur.

If a client is abusive to his or her lawyer (you might be surprised how often that happens) the lawyer is bound by attorney-client privilege and may not be able to extricate him or herself from representation if this happens mid-lawsuit. Bad behavior during litigation is protected by absolute immunity from suit. In other words, opposing counsel can defame, interfere with business, threaten, engage in all manner of offensive conduct that would otherwise subject them to a civil lawsuit, without fear of any consequence. The same applies to judges who have judicial immunity. State bars tasked with lawyer discipline are notoriously lenient and turn a blind eye to all kinds of abuse. Judicial commissions that look at judge conduct rarely take any action against judges. Lawyers and judges that fall apart from the pressure and succumb to alcohol or drug abuse or mental health problems are quietly provided treatment resources, but the existence of such rampant problems is pushed under the rug so as to not impugn the reputation of the profession as a whole.

Our entire governmental system is supposedly based on transparency and the right to comment on how our public officials do their jobs. Lawyers are considered officers of the court and thus, by extension, should also be held accountable to the public. Yet the general public has no idea what goes on in courtrooms every day, and they certainly have no clue (unless they have experienced it themselves) about the abuses that go on behind closed doors, in judges' chambers, in depositions, and in lawyers' offices.

Our founding fathers created a three-part governmental system: the legislative branch which creates laws, the executive branch which enforces them, and the judiciary branch which interprets laws and decides how they should be applied within the context of individual case facts. Each branch is designed to have checks and balances on and from the other branches of government. The media, sometimes referred to as the *fourth estate*, is supposed to keep a watchful eye on all of them. The judiciary branch, however, does its level best to minimize any watchful eye on its operations.

It is little wonder that the public distrusts lawyers. Secrets breed distrust, especially when something bad happens in a court case. However, lawyers are bound to a conspiracy of silence about even the most fundamental things that happen daily in their world.

No record is kept of the bulk of communications that occur in courtrooms and depositions. Experts[1] say that 55% of communication consists of body language, 38% is tone and inflection, and 7% is the actual words spoken. Because video and audio recording is banned in almost every court, the judicial system only keeps a record of the 7% via a court reporter transcribing proceedings and no record of the accompanying 93% of communication. When you factor in off-the-record conversations that are not transcribed at all, and add in translation of legal proceedings into another language and back (something that is never recorded), I would estimate that only 2% of the actual communication in our courts is recorded. That recording (written transcripts taken down by court reporters), and a pile of argumentative documents in the court file, stands for the whole truth of what happens in court cases. Some courtrooms are even eliminating the use of court reporters for motion hearings to save costs. Recently I had the experience where the official Minute Order in the court file was dramatically different from the actual events in the courtroom; it reflected that a defendant had waived an important Constitutional right when, in fact, the defendant did not waive this right at all.

Despite all of our high tech capabilities, court hearings have turned into a transient, visceral experience with few people present to witness it or hope to understand. There is less memorializing of what happens in court proceedings than social media records what people ate for dinner.

It astounds me that people get so upset about religious-charged symbols being located in or on courthouses. That should be the least of their worries. They should be more concerned about this sign posted at every courthouse:

No cameras

or recording

devices

Why are no cameras or recording devices allowed in courtrooms? Many excuses are given such as privacy of parties and dignity of the courtroom, but in truth, judges don't want anyone to second guess or armchair quarterback what happens in their courtrooms. Judges rule their own fiefdoms.

Furthermore, why are video cameras in depositions allowed to point at no one other than the person being deposed? All of the other intimidation and crazy dynamics of deposition are thinly recorded in a black and white transcript.

Lawyers labor in the dark world of their secrets, day in and day out, and it takes its secret toll. This book will shed a little light into the darkness.

HELPFUL HACK

File a written request for permission to record your court proceedings with an unobtrusive recording device (perhaps your cell phone). Although the courts usually only get these requests from media, they should get used to receiving them from ordinary citizens who just want a record of what is going on in their own case.

Why Lawyers Suck!

SHOWER, SHAVE,
AND VOMIT

*If success is not on your own terms, if it looks good
to the world but does not live in your heart,
it is not success at all.*

-Anna Quindlen

To the outsider, the world of lawyers is prestigious and important and, to some extent, even awe-inspiring. Even the mere stated intention that one intends to go to law school carries with it a certain "Wow, you must be really smart!" impression among friends and family. Why is this? Because lawyers and law schools have carefully crafted that image over the centuries and, aided by Hollywood and the media, the fiction persists.

The reality of the practice of law is far from its image. As one of my law professors told me, "You'll get one Perry Mason moment in your legal career. That's it." She was right. That blissful moment when you are questioning a witness in court and they break down and confess to everything on the witness stand, vindicating your client and making you, the attorney, feel like the brilliant hero. My law professor was right. I had my Perry Mason moment in my first year of practice. I got a 14-year-old boy to confess on the witness stand that he was the brains behind a school vandalism adventure and that my client, another teenage boy, had only reluctantly participated. The dramatic thrill of being a courtroom lawyer has been, in some respects, all downhill since then.

Early in my career I was having dinner with a lawyer I had just met. We shared war stories about our various cases, you know, the stuff that lawyers usually talk about, but after a glass or two of wine, he started opening up more. Every morning he would get up for work, shower, shave, and then throw up. Every morning. Shower, shave, vomit, put an expensive necktie noose around his neck, and go off to work a 16-hour day. He was young, mid-20s, and this was his life.

Sadly, his experience is more typical than not. As a young lawyer, I didn't vomit, but I did develop a dry heaving routine practically every afternoon of my workday. It was awful. At the time I was building up my criminal defense and juvenile law practice in Lincoln, Nebraska and at the same time moonlighting three days a week as a special prosecutor for crimes against children on the nearby Omaha Indian Reservation. This was after I had spent a year or so as a Deputy Public Defender. Within several years of practice I had seen awful things, things that no sane person should ever have to see. I had seen teenage girls pimped out by their parents for drug money, a victim of domestic assault begging me to represent the husband who had just hours before held a knife to her throat, a videotape of a sexual assault, autopsy photos of a young woman who had been beaten to death by her boyfriend in a drunken rage, and I had watched the autopsy of a child. If it were possible, I would pay millions of dollars to erase some of the images I have viewed because it was my job and now they can never be erased from my memory.

Sometimes I could justify the horror I had to see by believing I was doing justice, supporting the Constitution, all of that stuff. But honestly, that can only go so far. My body instinctively rebelled, trying just as desperately to expel all of those terrible things as it would have expelled the contents of my stomach from food poisoning.

One day several years into my legal practice, I happened to have a dictaphone in my car (I did a lot of commuting those days) and started dictating about my current life. There was something about the dynamic of just talking as I drove down that Southern California freeway that unleashed an honesty I hadn't had with myself before. I couldn't believe the things pouring out of my mouth, the dysfunction that was going on in my brain. As painful as it is to even read this now so many years later, here is what I said—

> I was born a quiet, sensitive and shy child, yet I find myself at the age of 33 in a harsh, male-dominated profession where the show of emotion equals weakness and weakness equals defeat. I am the worst of the worst. A shark. A trial lawyer. Every day I read police reports detailing the vile atrocities perpetrated by one human being against another. I talk to clients whose crimes are so heinous that society has chosen to lock them up for years. I hear them detail their crimes, their sexual perversions, and their intent to inflict revenge on those they deem responsible for their present incarceration. Although I know I should be completely revolted, running from their presence with my hands over my ears, I listen, enthralled.

No one can continue practicing law in such a manner forever. For every year of practice, there is another layer of disconnection that is essential for one to continue doing one's job. As a client, if you think your lawyer seems uncaring or just not as worked up about the problem facing you as you are, understand that he or she has seen it all and worse before. Where you may be jaded about the legal system and upset with what your legal problems have done to you, you will eventually be done and move on to other things. For the lawyer, it is just more of the same, day in day out, no end in sight. That is why the rates of suicide, depression, substance abuse, divorce and domestic problems are so rampant in the legal profession.

> If you think your lawyer seems uncaring, understand that he or she has seen it all and worse before.

Lawyers are three times more likely to suffer from depression than other professions, *twice* as likely to abuse substances as the general population, and *six times* more likely to commit suicide. Suicide is tenth on the top ten leading causes of death in the US, but the third leading cause of death among lawyers, behind only cancer and heart disease.[2]

HELPFUL HACK

Lawyers are especially adept at hiding substance abuse problems. He/she is unlikely to admit it is affecting their work until something bad has happened. Don't take a chance that it's something bad happening to your legal case. If you see signs of impairment in your lawyer, do not ignore them. Discuss your concerns with a supervising attorney, staff member, or the lawyer directly. If they are impaired, find another lawyer you can rely on. Your lawyer's clarity of mind is more important than their years of experience. Many lawyers are functional drunks or addicts for a long time and are unlikely to admit it is affecting their work until something bad has happened. If you see signs of potential impairment in your lawyer, do not ignore it. Discuss your concerns with a supervising attorney, staff member, or the lawyer directly. If they are impaired, find another lawyer you can rely on. Clarity of mind is more important than years of experience.

Some years ago I sat in a conference room with five other lawyers awaiting the start of the meeting. It was a uniquely diverse group by gender, age, type of law practice, time practicing law, and even a second career lawyer. As we chit-chatted before the meeting started, a single commonality emerged between us. We all disliked our jobs. It wasn't active hate, the type that motivates you to do anything to change your situation, just a deep and profound dissatisfaction with our careers and resignation to the fact that none of us had the prospect of ever knowing anything different.

It was in another law office several years later, however, that another lawyer summed up the situation of most lawyers more eloquently than I ever could. This lawyer, I'll call him James, was a lawyer I had never met before and he was rendering some legal advice to me. I actually had a certain level of envy for him as I waited for my appointment. His scope of practice seemed less stressful and more financially rewarding than my own. He had a nice-looking office, meticulous paperwork, one squared-away sample of a successful lawyer. As we were wrapping up our meeting, he gazed wistfully out the window. "You know, before going to law school I thought about opening an ice cream shop," he said. "Some days I just wish I could see people's faces light up as I handed them ice cream." I'll admit, that struck a nerve. There's a look that people get in their eyes when they learn I'm a lawyer. It's a look of fear, that even though they may have known me for awhile, the cloud of lawyerliness warrants an involuntary concern for their wellbeing. Sometimes I wish I could run an ice cream shop, too.

We are still lawyers, though, feeling helpless, I suspect, and unable to change career course now that we have committed so much money, time, blood, sweat and tears into it already.

As I write this book I have received a continual stream of responses back from lawyers giving almost unanimous support for this project. Here's an email I got from one young attorney that I am quoting with her permission.

I know I should read more about your book before I send this, but it's been a long day and I won't vent too much. I found your link because I was searching "lawyers suck blog." I'm a lawyer and I had a terribly frustrating day dealing with just the kind of lawyer that makes all of the lawyer jokes seem true. I've only been practicing three years, but I've seen such dishonorable actions by attorneys that it makes me not even want to bother anymore. There is no real fear of the ethics board, and the worst offenders seem to have no shame. Judges aren't willing to crack down and call them on the petty games, so clients on both sides just continue to get screwed.

They lecture us in law school about ethics and how we need to be a self-policing profession, but unless it has to do with stealing money, it doesn't seem as though anyone is being told to stop acting like a jerk and expect more of yourself and each other.

Is there any hope for our profession?

Maybe. If I didn't think there was any hope, you wouldn't have this book in your hands. Meaningful change, however, will only come when the legal profession stops creating lawyers that suck. K. Randolph of Voter Vault, aptly summed up the problem:

> "It's not that I hate people who are lawyers. … They can be giving, caring, compassionate, sincere, and trustworthy people. But … put them through four years of legal training, stick a suit on them, throw them in front of a judge, and they turn into the spawn of Satan."[3]

There is indeed "something wrong" with these people; they are trained to be what they are as you will see in the forthcoming chapters.

Meanwhile, however, there are some ways for you to evaluate whether your lawyer is in a good place mentally to handle your legal matters. After all, you are usually hiring a lawyer for his or her intellect, not joie de vivre.

HELPFUL HACK

Before hiring a lawyer, find out what their interests and activities are outside of their legal practice. If they have none, if they brag about being available to their clients 24/7 or routinely staying at the office until 7pm every night or later, that should be a red flag.

A clear mind, a well-functioning intellect, requires downtime and sleep, relaxation in between bouts of mental exertion. Fatigue leads to fuzzy thinking, inability to effectively solve problems, tasks taken longer than when one is well-rested, and, well, jerks. Select a lawyer or law firm who prioritizes mental health over workaholism, and you will get higher quality legal solutions.

HELPFUL HACK

If you are hiring a law firm, ask whether their associates have billable hour requirements. Do they have a quota per month or year? Most large law firms do, some requiring in excess of 2,000 billable hours a year. This is another red flag because you do not want to be paying for mere quota-filling hours.

THE ROAD TO HELL

"Easy is the descent into Hell,
for it is paved with good intentions."

-John Milton, Paradise Lost

Lawyers do not crawl up from primordial ooze onto dry land as you might suspect, but the process of selecting and grooming future lawyers is fundamentally flawed from the beginning. To get into law school, one needs to be fiercely competitive, be capable of suppressing human compassion to focus on intellectual thought, and either have the money (or be willing to place themselves deeply in debt in exchange) for that coveted "J.D." after their names.

If you talk to aspiring lawyers, you will find that most have noble intent. They aren't greedy; they aren't heartless. They really want to do some good in the world and see a legal career as giving them that opportunity.

The genesis of my desire to become a lawyer came from several sources. As a young child I visited Washington DC and Williamsburg, Virginia. I was in awe of the founding fathers, creating a new country out of fervent ideals and creativity. Of the 55 delegates to the Constitutional Convention, 35 were lawyers or had legal training, including Thomas

Jefferson whom I particularly admired. In my mind, the practice of law was a noble profession.

> Most aspiring lawyers have noble intent.
> They aren't greedy; they aren't heartless.

My suitability for a legal career first entered my mind in the eighth grade. My social studies teacher read us legal case summaries and had us guess which side would win. In each of the examples I was alone in my guess of who the prevailing party should be, coming to a different conclusion from all the other students in the class. And I was right each time. Being "right" is a powerful feeling, being "right" while going against the crowd is an even more powerful feeling.

I was also inspired by my uncle, Wilfried Kramer, who loved to talk about legal cases with all their intricate facts and complex arguments. My Uncle Will was the closest connection I had to the legal profession. Although not a lawyer himself, he had worked up the ranks from a courtroom bailiff to Clerk of the Court for the California Court of Appeals, Third District, and was actively involved in efforts to improve California's appellate court procedures. For me, he epitomized the perfect blend of intellect and challenging thinking that drew me to the study of law.

Friends, family, and my school teachers, however, would likely speculate that my desire to be a lawyer was more fueled by my love of arguing. It's true that by high school and college I regularly challenged test scores by pointing out to the instructors that although I may have not provided the answers they expected, my answers were in fact accurate in response to their (sometimes poorly worded) test questions. My instructors usually responded with some version of "You ought to be a lawyer; you like arguing so much," but they usually changed the test scores anyway.

Over time I was drawn to the law for another reason—people were impressed when I told them I planned to go to law school. They were equally impressed with people who planned to go to medical school, but frankly that was too much science and math and eventual blood and guts for me. By just *planning* to go to law school, I could get away with majoring in anything I wanted (I chose music) because there is no required pre-law program. Identifying myself as a future law school student provided me with an aura of being smart and driven. These are things I considered myself to be anyway, but it was nice to get external confirmation. Not a very outgoing person anyway, I found awe power to be a nice side benefit to my future plans.

My story is similar to that of many other lawyers. Having spoken with many lawyers, and numerous others interested in becoming lawyers, at least 9 times out of 10, their reasons are genuine and worthwhile, or at least not sinister. Few go down the road to law school only with the thought of becoming rich. That desire tends to come later.

Not everyone can be a lawyer, of course. There are limited seats in law school classes, and thus screening criteria decides who, among the many applicants, can begin legal studies. Getting into a law school, and thus starting the path to becoming a lawyer, is strewn with barriers that have nothing to do with honorable intentions nor with skill sets that lawyers should have. Only the strongest and most driven survive the process.

The first step to law school application is taking the Law School Admissions Test (LSAT). This is a standardized test administered by the Law School Admission Council and a prerequisite to seeking admission in any U.S. law school. The LSAC has a monopoly over this testing process. Every single American Bar Association approved law school is a member.

The problem with the LSAT should be readily apparent to any outsider, but seems to miss the grasp of the entire legal training machine—the LSAT tests for skills needed in law school[4], *not* those needed for the everyday practice of law. That's right. Potential law school students are screened for how well they will survive the peculiar, three-year, environment called law school. Being a genuine, caring person, having good business skills, or effective interpersonal interaction skills, do not even factor into the equation.

Law school exams are typically given at the end of each semester in law school, or a total of six sets of exams in the entirety of law school. A high LSAT score (which will give a student a more competitive edge when applying to law schools) demonstrates the likelihood of competitive ability in taking those six exams only.

With a high enough score on the LSAT, and then being selected out of a large pool of law school candidates, prospective lawyers begin their studies into all of the facets of being a lawyer . . . well, that is what they think they are being taught. In reality, they are being taught little about the everyday work of lawyers.

It didn't take long into my first year of law school to understand that many fundamental components were missing in our legal education. I wasn't the only one who noticed it; everyone commented on it. Law school does not teach students to *be* lawyers, nor to take the bar examination that is the prerequisite to getting a license to practice law. Law school only teaches students to *think like* lawyers. This leaves them completely unprepared to actually practice their profession within the context of real people and the real world. In response to law students' concerns on this point, professors and career counselors were quick to claim that those other skills would be taught by our law firm after we got our first associate job. That may have been the case many decades ago, but is not a reasonable expectation within the current legal job market and oversaturation of lawyers.

It is not *inside* of law school where lawyers get their bad reputations, it is *outside*. Lawyers get a bad reputation as they interact with the world outside of law school, something that is scarcely, if ever, addressed in pre-law school admission screening and is scarcely considered during law school. The screening criteria for prospective lawyers is for people who are good on paper only, good with complicated analysis entirely disconnected from the people whose daily lives are affected by the actions of lawyers. Law schools select and admit good test-takers. Thus begins the great divide between legal education and the practice of law, the beginning of the irrationality and lack of common sense you have witnessed in lawyers that prompted you to buy this book.

> Prospective lawyers are selected for law school because they are good on paper and good with complicated analysis—two things that are entirely disconnected from people whose lives will one day be affected by their actions.

A discussion of law school cannot be complete without a short discussion about the financial side of legal education. Law students embark on the path to lawyerhood with an unreasonable cost-benefit analysis of lawyering.

Anyone with basic business experience knows that before you invest your time and hard-earned money into a new venture, you should draw up a business plan. You should commit to paper what you are trying to accomplish, how you will go about it, what the market is like, potential risks and barriers to success, and, of course, the all-important financial projections. This process is key to understanding whether your planned endeavor has a reasonable chance of success, and whether the projected financial outcome is an acceptable return on investment for you and for any bank or investor willing to invest in your future success.

What if potential law students were required to submit a viable business plan as a prerequisite to getting student loans? The prospective lawyer would set forth his or her business goals, outline the investment capital required (tuition, living expenses while in school, etc.), the plan for starting gainful employment after graduating and getting a law license, the potential risks and barriers (not graduating in the top 10% of the law school class, downturn in associate hiring rates, excessive hours and stress limiting career length), and the all-important financials showing how and when the investment would be paid and what return on investment could be expected. The bookies in Vegas would drool with their odds that if this process were put in place, law school applications would drop by at least 50% in the first year, if not more. Either the prospective student would see the lack of financial sense to their overall plan, or the student loan lender would not approve of the plan.

This is what a business plan from a law student might look like.

Executive Summary

I plan to become a lawyer in the State of New York, get a high-paying associate position at a prominent law firm in Manhattan, pay off my student loans within the first 1-2 years, and live happily ever after.

Nature of Business

Upon graduation, I will specialize in business or corporate law, or anything else that sounds appealing upon graduation from law school. I will be paid as an employee by some prestigious law firm, get good benefits, and nice bonus checks every year.

The Industry

The need for lawyers has existed and grown over the centuries, and smart, driven, hardworking lawyers who graduate from Ivy League schools will never lack for work. The AmLaw 100 is a yearly list of the most prestigious law firms in the country, and I will only work for one of them.

Business Objectives

I intend to have an intellectually stimulating and exciting job. I will own a BMW, have a trophy spouse to bring to the firm's annual picnic, join a country club, and live happily ever after.

Financial Projections

Capital investments will be the cost of law school tuition, books, fees, living expenses during law school, and plenty of beer money. That lasts for three years. Then for the following several months after graduation, there will be costs for a bar review prep course, the cost of taking the bar exam, and living expenses while spending night and day studying for the bar exam. Then living expenses for another couple of months to catch up on my sleep and start frantically looking for a job while I await receipt of my bar results for months, even though most employers will want to make sure I passed the bar exam first.

No revenue of any consequence is anticipated during those 3-1/2 years because there is no time to work between classes, homework, and exams, and furthermore, most law schools strictly limit any work while attending law school.

Beginning associate salaries at large law firms are reported in legal journals as being $100K-$150K which is so much more money than I've ever made before that I'm sure I will easily be able to pay all my bills, drive a nice car, go on lavish vacations, and pay off my student loans within a year or two.

Risks and Barriers

As long as I study really, really hard and get in the top 10% of my law school class, I'm set. I'm smart; I'm driven; this should not be a problem.

Neither purveyors of student loans, nor the law schools that reap the benefit of tuition payments, care that such a plan is downright irresponsible and near-sighted. Take that plan to a potential investor with even a small amount of sophistication and they would laugh (politely or impolitely) and decline to invest.

> Neither purveyors of student loans, nor the law schools that reap the benefit of tuition payments, care that investment in a law school education is often downright irresponsible and near-sighted.

So why do thousands of would-be lawyers proceed to take out student loans and invest in law school? Legal education in the US is very expensive. Most students emerging from law school these days are stooping under the weight of a $100K+ student loan burden. They (and their law schools) justify incurring such debt by saying that it will prepare them for a profession that will pay more than enough to cover these loan payments. Newspaper stories talking about $300, $500, $900/hr billable rates for lawyers, and seeing *starting* associate salaries advertised at well over $120K, buttresses that belief. However, the reality of earning power for lawyers is not as bright as advertised, especially in recent years. Large numbers of highly qualified lawyers with impeccable academic credentials are unable to get work after law school graduation, or are only able to find jobs paying salaries that are insufficient to justify the massive student loan payments. This problem has become so serious that in recent years many law school graduates have sued their law schools claiming that the law schools provided deceptive employment data and defrauded them.

Having independent wealth will help a lawyer avoid at least one pitfall of the costs of legal education; it may act as a buffer to protect one's law license during tough financial times. In 2009 a young lawyer saddled with hundreds of thousands of dollars of law school debt lost his bar license *because* he had so much debt. The Texas appeals court, in upholding the bar's decision, raised the *possibility* that the lawyer would harm a client, obstruct administration of justice or violate disciplinary rules. There was no mention that the lawyer *had* done any of these things, just that he *might* due to debt. Had this unfortunate young lawyer had independent wealth to pay his way through law school, he would still have his bar license.

⌐ HELPFUL HACK

If you are an aspiring lawyer looking to get into law school, evaluate your plans as you would if you were investing in a business. Put together a business plan similar to the one outlined here, and include realistic goals and financials that match your plans. If you want to be a lawyer to do good in the world through a non-profit or low-income producing job, factor that into your financial planning. You don't need a high-priced law school if that is the case. You'll need a solid legal education from a quality law school. Trust me, when it comes to lawyering, higher tuition will not make you better prepared to perform legal tasks for your clients. If you want to be a "pedigreed" lawyer from an expensive law school, then make sure your financial plan accounts for the high risk that you will not easily (or at all) get a job that will generate enough income for you to get a reasonable return on your investment of time and money.

ERODING OF HUMANITY

"A lawyer who shares his client's pain, in my opinion, does his client such a grave disservice, he should have his license to practice law taken away. It clouds his judgment. And that's as beneficial to his client as a doctor who recoils at the sight of blood."

-*Jan Schlichtmann* (played by John Travola in the movie "A Civil Action")

One complaint I received while I was working on this book was that "lawyers are unable to connect with others on a human level." The selection of lawyers by their skills on paper vs. real life skills is certainly part of the cause of this, but there's more to it than that.

The first time I questioned a witness in a courtroom was during my third year of law school. I was clerking in the local prosecutor's office at the time. Along with a deputy prosecutor to supervise, I was handling an evidentiary hearing regarding whether a 16-year-old arrested with burglary tools would be tried as an adult or as a juvenile. The stakes were high. If prosecuted as a juvenile, the worst that could happen would be that he would be sent to a juvenile detention facility until he aged out at 18, at which point he would probably embark on an active criminal career. He had already been in a lot of legal trouble in his short life and had already spent time in a juvenile detention facility. On the other hand, if prosecuted as an adult, he could be facing 10 years in prison.

With the mentor attorney at my side, I felt well-prepared for what I needed to do. I had been given a list of essential questions to be asked of both witnesses, the juvenile's probation officer (whom I had already talked with at length) and the juvenile's mother (who I was sure would argue that her son should be treated as a juvenile).

The questioning of the probation officer went without incident. He even volunteered an answer he knew I needed before I asked the question. Then the juvenile's mother took the stand. Now having a child of my own, I have a new appreciation of how gut-wrenchingly awful this must have been for her to even be there in court, knowing the serious trouble her son was in, knowing that her testimony may be a key factor in what would happen to him next.

I patiently waited while the juvenile's lawyer walked the mother through his own questions. She tearfully explained to the judge how her son was basically a good kid and how being prosecuted as an adult would ruin his life. I'm sure any mom would have done the same. Then it was my turn to do the questioning.

I did not doubt her sincerity, but my job was to point out the incompleteness of her testimony, putting facts before the judge that would result in permission for adult prosecution. I cross-examined the mother about her son's troubled past. There were more tears and admissions that he had been uncontrollable for years. I pointed out the inaccuracy of her claims that she would be able to monitor her son's actions. She admitted that since his recent release from juvenile detention he hadn't even been home and she did not know where he was staying. (I didn't know that for sure when I asked the questions, but I had a hunch, and it was right.) It was pretty clear that even a mother's fervent pleas for leniency on this issue were not going to be effective.

The judge issued the order from the bench to allow prosecution as an adult. Court adjourned.

I collected my files and walked out into the hallway, trying not to throw up. I had just used the power of my words to devastate a sincere, innocent mother who was trying to protect her child. Yes, protection of the public warranted the outcome in that courtroom, but I found no joy in it. "You did good," my mentor said, patting me on the shoulder. Seeing the look on my face, she added "You did the right thing."

My mentor was right, but she was also wrong. That day I lost my innocence, my unimpeded kind spirit in the presence of another human being in pain. I don't think it has ever fully come back. Now, over 20 years in, I easily "slice and dice" witnesses with cross-examination, making them concede the points I want them to make, making them say things they never intended to say, making them look like fools, and sometimes I reduce them to tears. It makes me an expert in my field, but it also makes me a jackass and a heartless human being. After awhile it gets hard to look yourself in the mirror.

> After 20 years, I easily "slice and dice" witnesses with cross-examination. It makes me an expert in my field, but it also makes me a jackass and a heartless human being.

Not every lawyer has such a dramatic shifting point in the eroding of their humanity. For others, the process occurs in smaller steps. The eroding of a lawyer's inherent sense of right and wrong and, at some point, their humanity, begins even before law school; even the LSAT begins that process.

One of the skills tested on the LSAT is the ability to distinguish a question as being one of law or one of fact. Here's an example.

Harriet is rushing through the grocery store with her three young children, trying to pick up the last few things she needs for dinner, worried that there won't be enough time for both homework and baths tonight. While she turns to pick up a head of lettuce, little Joey grabs a banana and as he gets ready to stuff it into his mouth, the banana peel falls to the floor right in front of Harriet who promptly slips and falls, breaking her hip in the process.

Question. Will the grocery store be responsible to pay for Harriet's medical bills?

In responding to that question on the LSAT, keep in mind that nobody cares about Harriet writhing in pain on the floor, nobody cares that the kids don't end up getting any dinner until hours later, nobody cares that her husband who is working the late shift at the factory must hurry over to the ER to pick up the hungry kids and get them fed, bathed, and homework done, losing a day's pay in the process. Nobody cares about the weeks and months of agonizing pain she suffers while trying to run the household and work at her job. That is unimportant. The answer, and only answer relevant to that question on the LSAT, would be identifying whether the question is one of fact or law. Is this a helpful skill? Sure, it is, and important for lawyers. It begins a slippery slope, however, of disregarding reality of pain in others in favor of strict intellectual arguments.

By the first year of law school, this process is taken a step further, testing aspiring lawyers' ability to disconnect their humanity in favor of academic arguments. Near the end of the first year of law school, students are required to participate in Moot Court. They are given a sample case, facts and law, and given a side to represent. In teams of two, they research the law and write an appellate brief to a fictional court. Then they present oral arguments to a panel of judges (often practicing lawyers or retired judges) and get graded and ranked on their brief writing and performance. There's a catch, though. You don't get to pick what side of the case you are on, and you have to be ready to argue the other side's position on a moment's notice.

⌐ HELPFUL HACK

If you are hiring a lawyer because you have been injured, understand that he or she will be looking at your problem in an objective sense— how can they get you money in exchange for your injury— not in a caring human being sense. Remember that this is their role; you have hired them to get money, not to be your best friend. Share your pain and frustration with a friend, colleague, or therapist, not your lawyer.

There are no slip-and-fall cases in Moot Court. The law school ups the ante. Can the law student set aside his or her deeply held moral principles and even argue against them? This process is the first direct testing of a law student's moral compass vs. their desire to practice law.

The selected mock case usually involves something controversial or hard to justify in your own mind. I believe I was assigned to defend a drug dealer who was caught with a suitcase full of cocaine. Sometimes it has to do with gay rights, or abortion, some polarizing topic. Without fail, a certain number of law students protest at this point in their law school process, saying they should not be forced to argue something they don't believe in. It happened when I was a first year law student in 1990-1991 at the University of Nebraska College of Law. It happened to Scott Turow, bestselling author of *One L,* in the mid-70s at Harvard Law School. It happens every year, in every law school in the country. However, almost 100% of the students end up caving. A few quit law school. Here's why.

This crisis of conscience moment comes near the end of a grueling first year of law school. You are tired, likely more exhausted than you have ever been in your life. You have spent more time reading and summarizing cases than you thought was possible to do without your eyes literally falling out of your head. You have missed time with your family and friends, stayed in the law library when you would otherwise been having an actual life, and you have likely put yourself in substantial debt already for tuition and living expenses. You have made a huge investment in your future of being a lawyer. You are competitive, and hardworking, and you do not want to be a quitter, you do not want to be derailed by taking a moral stand, however strongly you may feel about it. The instructors, publicly and privately, assure you that this is what law students are required to do, the problem was chosen well in advance and will not be changed and you can do the exercise or pack your bags. So you do it. You vigorously and thoroughly argue something you do not believe in, and compete with your fellow law students to do it better than all of them.

⌐ HELPFUL HACK ⌐

Before you decry this moral caving of lawyers too much, understand that it will also enable a lawyer to argue on your behalf even if you haven't thoroughly convinced him or her of your position's moral worth.

It's hard the first time you do that. It's much easier the second time, and the third. . . .

Truth is, however, that it's hard to be in touch with your humanity while focusing on all the meticulous details of your job. It is often also counterproductive to your clients' interests. An excellent example of this is shown in the movie "A Civil Action" starring John Travolta.

In the movie, Travolta plays a powerful plaintiff's attorney called upon to represent families in a New England town whose water supply was being poisoned by a corporation's business operations nearby, causing the death of numerous children. It is based on a true story. The plaintiffs have been emotionally devastated by the loss of their children. Travolta's usually cynical and greedy character decides to take on the case and the battle is on between the lawyers and parties. Lawyer games, emotional depositions, lying witnesses, land surveys, expensive experts. Travolta's character comments that in civil litigation both parties keep spending unreasonable amounts of money and the first one to come to their senses, loses. In this case, with trial coming near, the defendant corporations summon the plaintiff's representatives for a settlement meeting. They propose a multi-million dollar settlement for the group of plaintiffs. Travolta begins a calm response, then completely flips out, demanding the offered dollar amount for each plaintiff instead of the group, in addition to costs of cleanup, and other expenses. In short, his emotional outburst regarding the settlement proposal makes settlement impossible and trial inevitable.

While the jury is deliberating on the first phase of the case, Travolta and one of the defendant corporation lawyers, played by Robert Duvall, are sitting in the courthouse hallway. Duvall pulls out a $20 dollar bill and lays it down on the bench between them and says "what if I were to add six zeros onto that" as a settlement proposal. Travolta won't take the deal and walks away.

By now, Travolta's character is emotionally involved in the case, demanding justice for the clients, irrespective of financial consequence to his law firm. The law firm's financial guy, William Macy, is arranging for lines of credit, second mortgages on partners houses, every credit card offer he can find, all in an effort to pay the costs of furthering the lawsuit. The law firm is going bankrupt because Travolta's character is proceeding under "the principle of the thing" concept. The partners are finally down to an unfurnished, unlit office and Travolta still doesn't want to settle. "This isn't about money anymore," he says and finally admits that the difference between a settlement amount he will take and won't take is "if they are willing to pay [it], then its not enough."

In the end, they finally have no choice but to accept a small settlement that will allow them to pay off the expenses incurred, IRS tax liens, and other debts. They reduce their attorney fees too, leaving $375,000 per family that they represented. The law firm partners drive up to meet with the families to explain the result and how much each family would get. The main plaintiff looks at Travolta's character and says "what I wanted was an apology." Here Travolta has given up everything for his clients, even his law firm, and the client's response is that they still weren't satisfied.

In Travolta's case, he was a lawyer entirely in touch with his humanity; his caring and concern for his clients was undeniable. Yet it was that humanity that cost him a much better case outcome.

Ironically, although Travolta's character could never be accused of being a heartless or uncaring lawyer, nothing he did or didn't do would have ultimately satisfied the clients. They weren't satisfied because what they wanted was something that could never be obtained in a courtroom— an apology.

There is no legal process in this country whereby we force litigants to utter the words "I'm sorry" to the other side. Perhaps we should. Parents do that all the time with squabbling children. I remember my mother making me apologize to my brother, and he to me, on innumerable occasions. Did we feel particularly sorry at the time? Probably not so much, but it impressed on us the importance of verbally acknowledging that we had done something wrong *to the party harmed.*

HELPFUL HACK

Before deciding to sue someone, you must, must, must step back and evaluate what you want to accomplish with the lawsuit. What outcome a year or more down the road are you hoping to have? Picture yourself at the end of the lawsuit, what you would have received that would make you feel better than you do now? Write it down. Then work backwards to see whether that outcome is even possible. Courts cannot bring back loved ones, cannot change the fact that you were injured, cannot make the other person apologize. If you think forcing the other side to write a big check would make you feel better, write down what you would do with the money. Next, decide how much time and money you are willing to commit to fighting for that outcome. There will be costs for filing fees, expert witnesses, document production, depositions. Even if the law firm is initially paying those costs, check your fee agreement, you may have to pay them at the end. In some cases there is even a risk that you might have to pay the other side's attorney fees and costs if you lose. There is also time and work you will have to incur in responding to discovery requests, collecting documents, perhaps having independent medical examinations, being deposed, court hearings, a trial. This is time you could be spending doing other things. When you have this list put together, set it aside for a few days before you make a final decision. Talk to your significant others about the pros and cons. Maybe, having considered all of these facts, you still want to proceed to file a lawsuit, but you are at least prepared for what sacrifices are involved and what you may get in exchange for your investment.

It is undeniable that a lawyer's humanity and sense of right and wrong is eroded over the course of time through legal education and practice, but in all fairness, that fact may have little to do with the public's dissatisfaction with lawyers. Unreasonable expectations cannot be met because they are unreasonable, not because the parties involved in the process are either good or bad. A lawsuit cannot bring back a loved one, it cannot heal an injured person, it cannot erase emotional harm, and in many cases, cannot even undo financial harm. It certainly cannot provide those intangible things that we, as intertwined human beings, really need when we have suffered some type of harm at the hands of another to find healing and move on with our lives in peace.

> There is no legal process in this country whereby we force litigants to utter the words "I'm sorry" to the other side. Perhaps we should.

LAWYERS CANNOT DO "SIMPLE"

Any darn fool can make something complex;
it takes a genius to make something simple.

-Pete Seeger

L awyers must be darn fools, because they cannot do "simple." They write documents that are too complicated to comprehend. They talk to people in such complex terms that no one can understand them. They call a 25-page document a "brief." Ironically (true confessions here) this section of the book was the hardest for me to write, it is the longest section, it is the only chapter with subsections, took forever to edit, and I'm still not satisfied with it. My struggle is a personal testimony to the fact that lawyers don't know how to do things in a simple or straightforward manner, even if they are really trying hard to do so.

Lawyers value complexity and ambiguity far more than simplicity. There are four primary reasons for this—

1. Lawyers are educated to find levels of complication in every situation;

2. The "law" becomes more and more complicated over time, by design;

3. Lawyers live and work within a complex and antiquated judicial system that is anything but simple; and

4. Lawyers lose sleep for fear of missing any detail.

Lawyers are trained to make everything complicated

Lawyers are trained to never take anything for granted, never view any position as the only correct one, and frankly, after a time, we get annoyed with those who cannot see the fine nuances and potential arguments, pro and con, in every single situation.

> For lawyers, nothing can be taken for granted, no position is the only correct one, and they can see the fine nuances and potential arguments in any situation.

Early in my married life my new husband joked with me that my answer to any "yes" or "no" question was usually "that depends." Its corollary, equally abhorrent to him, was the phrase "not necessarily."

In other words, I didn't seem capable of giving a straight answer to any question. "Is the sky blue?" "Well, that depends. Sometimes it's blue, different shades depending on where you are, what the weather is like, or the time of day. On cloudy days the sky is really shades of white and gray, and sometimes it looks red, or pink around sunset, or when there is a nearby fire . . ." I mean really, the possibilities are endless, to a lawyer. This becomes even more annoying to clients who are relying on their lawyers to help them make decisions that fundamentally affect their life. "Will I win my case?" "That depends."

In fairness, lawyers truthfully don't know "the answer" to anything; giving anything less than a firm "maybe" wouldn't be truthful. Based on the nature of the law (which changes daily), how it is researched, and how it is applied, a lawyer cannot be confident that any answer is ever "right."

The skill of "*issue spotting*"—finding every potential argument or factual wrinkle in any scenario—is crucial to both admittance and survival in law school. "Issue spotting" in layman's terms is taking a microscope to every problem so that more problems or ambiguities can be found. Something that appears to be simple on its face must be dissected and scrutinized until it becomes complicated and ambiguous, thus fodder for dispute.

Here's how "issue spotting" plays out in the context of drafting a contract (and one of the reasons why legal documents are so long).

John and Mary are neighbors who help each other out from time to time. When Mary decides to go on vacation, she asks John to take care of her dog while she's gone, and he agrees. She promises that, in exchange for him helping out, she'll bake him one of her famous apple pies. They memorialize this agreement between them on a cocktail napkin. It reads as follows:

I, John, agree to feed Mary's dog Buster while she is away on vacation.

In exchange, Mary will bake me an apple pie.

Signed June 4, 2015

John   *Mary*

Although John and Mary are not thinking in these terms, this handwritten document has all the elements necessary to be an enforceable contract. John agreed to do something (take care of the dog); Mary agreed to give him something in exchange (bake him a pie); they both agreed to the same thing; and the agreement had a legal purpose.

Is there ambiguity in this agreement? John and Mary don't think so, but any competent lawyer or even law student will see it is full of holes, ambiguities, and has room for misunderstandings and disputes. For example, what are John's responsibilities here really? If he feeds Buster once while Mary is gone, has he fulfilled his obligations? Mary would not think so (and Buster, of course, would also heartily disagree if he could talk). Maybe, just to be sure, this agreement could be a little more precise. And, while we're at it, perhaps we should add last names to make this a little more formal. Here are the edits in redlined fashion.

I, John Brown, agree to feed Mary Smith's dog, Buster, every morning and every evening while Mary Smith ~~she~~ is away on vacation. In exchange, Mary Smith will bake John Brown ~~me~~ an apple pie when Mary Smith ~~she~~ returns from vacation.

Signed June 4, 2015

John Brown   *Mary Smith*

There, much better. But, you know, this doesn't specify when Mary is going to be away on vacation. Maybe it will be the same time that John was planning to be on vacation and that wouldn't work at all. Maybe feeding the dog for a week is fine, but what if Mary decides to stay away a month? Is that still okay? Oh, and that apple pie. When will it be delivered? The day Mary returns from vacation? Sometime in the year following the dog feeding? I mean, if John isn't going to get a pie for a year, is it really worth the responsibility of caring for the dog? And what about that apple pie? Does Mary mean a basic apple pie, which is good, or is she promising to use that special recipe with the streusel topping and drizzle of caramel? Maybe the agreement needs a few more details, to remove these ambiguities.

> I, John Brown, agree to feed Mary Smith's dog, Buster, every morning and every evening while Mary Smith ~~she~~ is away on vacation. Said vacation is scheduled for July 1— 8, 2015. If Mary Smith wants to change the dates of her vacation for purposes of this agreement, she must get prior consent from John Brown. In exchange, Mary Smith will bake John Brown ~~me~~ an apple pie, specifically Mary Smith's Special Family Secret Recipe Struesel and Caramel Apple Pie within one week of ~~when~~ Mary Smith's ~~she~~ returns from vacation.

> Signed June 4, 2015

> *John Brown*   *Mary Smith*

Now Mary starts looking at it a little closer, you know, to make sure that her interests are adequately covered. What is John going to feed the dog anyway? The gourmet dog feed she usually feeds him, or the crappy, inexpensive food he feeds his own dogs? Better make sure it's the right food. And what if something happens to poor Buster during the week she is gone? He's not a pup anymore after all. If Buster is collapsed on the bedroom floor and needs emergency vet care, will she really feel that John is taking care of him by just putting out a bowl of food? Absolutely not! That is not good enough for her Buster. And what is that about so severely limiting her vacation dates? What if she decides to stay an extra day, or leave a day early? Really? She has to check in with John to get "permission" to alter her vacation dates? More editing needs to be done.

> I, John Brown, agree to take care of ~~feed~~ Mary Smith's dog, Buster, while she is away on vacation as scheduled below. "Taking care of" Buster includes, but is not limited to the following: (1) feeding Buster every morning and every evening with Extra Special Gourmet Dog Food; (2) ensuring that Buster has not suffered any accident or other health problem during the duration of the vacation; and (3) taking appropriate actions to care for the health and well-being of Buster, if necessary, taking him to the vet. ~~while Mary Smith she is away on vacation~~. Said vacation is scheduled for July 1-8, 2015. If Mary Smith wants to change the dates of her vacation for purposes of this agreement, she must get prior consent from John Brown, which consent shall not be unreasonably withheld. In exchange, Mary Smith will bake John Brown ~~me~~ an apple pie, specifically Mary Smith's Special Family Secret Recipe Struesel and Caramel Apple Pie within one week of ~~when~~ Mary Smith's ~~she~~ returns from vacation.

Signed June 4, 2015

John Brown   Mary Smith

John looks at the new agreement. Really? I've owned dogs for four decades. I certainly wouldn't let a sick dog just lay on the floor for days. I would take Buster to the vet, but Mary has to pay the bill. And I'm not driving across town to the spa-inspired vet office Mary uses; I'm going to the neighborhood vet who is just as good, but charges half the price. Now, as to the food thing, fine, as long as Mary is stupid enough to pay twice as much money as she needs to on fancy dog food for her precious dog (there's just an unhealthy connection between those two; Mary needs to find herself a boyfriend) that's fine, but I'm not buying it. That's her responsibility. And seriously, for all of this, I want more than one apple pie. I want a pie a week for the next month. More editing is needed.

> I, John Brown, agree to take care of ~~feed~~ Mary Smith's dog, Buster, while she is away on vacation as scheduled below. "Taking care of" Buster includes, but is not limited to the following: (1) feeding Buster every morning and every evening with Extra Special Gourmet Dog Food (said food will be provided by Mary at her expense); (2) ensuring that Buster has not suffered any accident or other health problem during the duration of the vacation (limited to any health problem reasonably observable by John Brown upon his twice daily visits to feed Buster; John Brown shall not be responsible to check on Buster any more frequently than that); and (3) taking appropriate actions to care for the health and well-being of Buster (within the bounds of reason, in the sole discretion of John Brown), if necessary, taking him to the vet (the choice of vet being made by John Brown at his sole discretion, and any expenses will be reimbursed in full by Mary Smith immediately upon her return from vacation regardless of the outcome of any such treatment). ~~while Mary Smith~~

~~she is away on vacation.~~ <u>Said vacation is scheduled for July 1-8, 2015. If Mary Smith wants to change the dates of her vacation for purposes of this agreement, she must get prior consent from John Brown, which consent shall not be unreasonably withheld.</u> In exchange, Mary <u>Smith</u> will bake <u>John</u> Brown ~~me an~~ <u>four</u> apple pie<u>s, specifically Mary Smith's Special Family Secret Recipe Struesel and Caramel Apple Pie, one per week commencing within seven (7) days of</u> ~~within one week of when~~ Mary Smith's ~~she~~ returns <u>from vacation, and continuing on a weekly basis until all four pies have been delivered.</u>

Signed June 4, 2015

John Brown   *Mary Smith*

You may be laughing or shaking your head, but this dynamic plays itself out every single day in lawyers' lives. I remember one contract that the parties edited back and forth for over one year. The parties met in person to negotiate a deal over a business dispute. There were seven or eight of us, parties and attorneys from each side. Each side made their case for their position, the other side responded back. Huddles of each side were interspersed with group conversations. After about six hours a deal was struck. A term sheet was prepared and signed, everyone shook hands. Mission accomplished. Then the attorneys started hammering out the specific contract language. Each draft was responded to with a new round of changes and modifications. Phone calls went back and forth and back and forth. Finally, over a year after the handshakes, a final contract was signed. In fairness to the lawyers, this wasn't just idle arguing. Many of the terms being hammered out had the potential to materially change the overall value of the deal to one side or the other, and neither wanted to diminish the benefit of the bargain they had struck.

At least this year-plus contract finalization process had some substance to it. That is not always the case. Lawyers engage in the same type of vehement back and forth for even tiny, inconsequential details, because lawyers don't know when to stop. I'll never forget a battle over a joint report to be filed with the court where my co-counsel and the opposing attorney had a huge argument just hours before the deadline whether a certain sentence should be in **bold** or *italics*.

HELPFUL HACK

Some transactions warrant an extremely detailed agreement, and some don't. Before you decide whether to hire a lawyer to prepare a meticulous contract that covers every possible scenario and outcome, evaluate the size of risk if something goes wrong with the relationship. Does this contract involve a lot of money? A lengthy period of time? Will something bad happen if either you or the other side back out of their obligations? Scale the level of detail to your specific needs and budget and explain this to your lawyer.

The ultimate prize for such frivolity is awarded to a lawyer whose identity I will not disclose. I had been working with the attorney on a joint document to be filed with the Court. The case had been very contentious for months, and this report was no exception, but we were down to the final details, and after accepting his last round of changes, I thought we were done. It was Friday afternoon and I wanted to get out of the office. So, I went ahead and electronically filed the document with the Court and headed out the door. I hadn't even gotten home yet when I got a call from my paralegal. Opposing counsel had emailed and was livid! How dare I file the document without his final approval?! I called him back and explained that I had just accepted his most recent changes and made no more edits of my own so I didn't think he needed to review it again. I told him to feel free to review it again and, if there were any problems, I would take care of withdrawing my filing and refiling a corrected version. Several hours later I got an email with his "changes." He wanted to fix the signature block. Here's what was wrong with the signature block—

   \s\Crazy Attorney   instead of   \s\Crazy Attorney

Before you go cross-eyed trying to figure out the difference, I'll tell you. The first two spaces of my signature line used the underline key while the rest of the line used the underline format function, resulting in an ever-so-slightly lower line for the first two spaces.

┌─ HELPFUL HACK ─┐

Abolish hourly rate contracts whenever possible because lawyers can spend an endless amount of time on any project. The only limitations will be the amount of money that a client will pay. Put limitations on the amount of time spent on certain tasks, or flat fee task pricing. If a law firm gets a flat fee of $2,000 for each motion written, you can bet that the lawyers will not spend 20 hours on it.

It was that day that I stopped hating opposing counsel on that case. All I felt was pity. How terrible it must be going through life that way? I was enjoying a sunny afternoon while he was dissecting the most minor of typography differences that made no difference to the substance of the document, our clients, or the Court.

Lawyers' environment does nothing to help this problem of not knowing when to stop editing. It is hard not to develop obsessive compulsive behaviors when the infrastructure within which lawyers work is barely above the Stone Age in efficiency or logic, and yet it is governed by the most meticulous sets of rules.

The "law" becomes more and more complicated over time, by design

You would assume that lawyers know a lot about what "the law" is about various topics and, if they practice long enough, they should know pretty much all of the laws. Unfortunately, the American legal system is designed such that it is impossible for any one person, or any one law firm, or any one army of people, to ever get a handle on it. It's like one of those sci-fi creatures that keeps growing limbs and spawning replicas of itself until they take over the entire world.

> The law is like one of those sci-fi creatures that keeps growing limbs and spawning replicas of itself until they take over the entire world.

On this topic, I give law schools credit for honesty. They don't even pretend to be teaching students "the law." In the first year, law students are taught to "think like lawyers" and how to "find the law." In the second year of law school, you learn advanced skills of "interpreting the law." The rest of the time is spent talking about legal decisions, arguing over laws, and wondering whether when you get out of law school you will even know how to find a courthouse. Other than that, you are on your own. You will never, ever, ever, feel confident that you know "the law" on any given topic and at any given time, because it constantly changes and grows larger.

The basics learned in the first year of law school are that "the law" consists of primary legal sources (the Constitution, statutes, municipal codes, etc.), caselaw (decisions of court cases that interpret those laws in the context of specific disputes between parties), and a bunch of other stuff that talks about legal stuff (like law review articles, legal newspapers, legal reference books, legislative history, and frankly anything else that might help out your arguments). As a lawyer, you need to learn how to find and weave together all of these pieces into a cohesive whole, whether you are arguing a case in court or advising a client.

When I was in law school, I practically lived in the law library. I studied there; I worked there; I sometimes even dozed off with my head atop a pile of books. Before every law school exam I ritually rubbed the nose of the Roscoe Pound[5] bust sitting at the library entrance for luck. Yet, I didn't ever feel like I "knew" the law. It was too overwhelming to ever firmly grasp, even if it didn't regularly change. There was a library upstairs called the tax library. No kidding, two full rooms of books containing some of the tax laws. I'll confess, I didn't even try to learn tax law. Sorry, Professor Lyons, my amazing tax professor, advisor, and mentor, you did your best.

Despite all the books, "the law" is an ever-changing, living organism. As to the United States Constitution, it's pretty constant. It's been around since 1789 and, though it has had 33 amendments since then, its not really hard to keep track of its contents. Federal statutes? Well, they change all the time. Frankly, I think Congress ought to sit out a few terms without passing any new laws, just to see if all the ones already there can work for awhile. There are 54 titles (or sections) of the

United States Code on topics ranging from national parks, to patriotic ceremonies, navigation, Indians, copyrights, court procedures, flags, aliens, and foreign relations. Each of those titles has subtitles and innumerable sections underneath. They are complicated and sometimes imprecise, so for more detail you can refer to the legislative history (what Congressional representatives talked about before passing the legislation), or the Code of Federal Regulations (CFR) which provides yet more detail of what you can and cannot do and what may, may not, or might happen if you do, or don't do …Then every state has its own laws, statutes passed by its own legislature. None are alike, though some have overlaps or steal code sections from other states. I first noticed this habit of states using other states' statutes years ago when I wrote a prosecutor's manual for traffic offenses for the State of Nebraska. Now, if you are familiar with Nebraska, you will know that Nebraska is basically flat. There are some sand dunes out in the western part of the state, but there is nothing resembling a mountain. However, Nebraska's Traffic Code contains this gem:

> NRS 484B.120 Driving on defiles, canyons or moun-
> tain highways. The driver of a motor vehicle traveling
> through defiles or canyons or on mountain highways shall
> hold such motor vehicle under control and as near the right
> hand edge of the highway as reasonably possible.

"Defiles" is a rather antiquated word meaning a narrow pass or gorge, especially between two mountains . Now I couldn't just let that oddity go without researching a little further. I discovered that Nebraska copied Illinois's traffic code. Well, that didn't explain the mountain highways provision; Illinois is flatter than Nebraska. However, Illinois didn't write its own traffic code, it lifted its traffic code from Colorado, where there actually are canyons and mountainous highways. Mystery solved, sort of. I placed this little gem of information as a footnote in the Nebraska County Attorneys' Association's *The Prosecutor's Traffic Manual, 3rd Edition*, printed in 1994. It sits on the bookshelf of prosecutors and judges throughout the state. Nobody seems to have removed the nonsensical statute, though[6].

So, in addition to having all of that "law," courts have been deciding cases based on a couple of sources, (1) applicable primary sources of law (statutes, constitutions, for example); and (2) prior court decisions in similar cases (referred to as caselaw). This is referred to as a common law system, where the law builds upon itself over the years. In fact, American law builds on case decisions from England. Shocking, I know. Court decisions in 2015 can base their rationale on a case from the 1400s.

How many court case decisions exist upon which courts can rely? How big is this "pile" of caselaw, prior court decisions that courts must or may factor into their own decision? I'll be honest, I don't know where to find that kind of statistic. Over half a million cases are filed in federal and state courts in a year, that means well over 10 million cases filed since I graduated from law school. Even though only a small percentage of those cases result in a published case decision, the volume is enormous, constantly growing and never diminishing. Long ago, WestLaw, the largest publisher of caselaw, came up with an indexing system, a means of connecting the dots through the maze of caselaw, summarizing key elements of each case such that it can be cross-referenced with other cases involving the same or similar issues. That helps, a lot, but isn't enough. Caselaw changes over time, too. A court may have said X in 1960, but in 1982 the same court, under a different set of circumstances (and probably with a different mix of judges), decided that the decision in 1960 was wrong, and therefore you cannot rely on the 1960 case anymore. However, they don't rip those pages out of the caselaw books or databases; you just have to go through steps to check whether a case you want to rely on was overruled in this manner at any time since it was issued. There have been times when a relevant case decision was overturned while you are in the middle of your case.

Here's what we had to do when I was in law school to find and verify caselaw. You had to start with a topical index (digest) that organized cases by topics. This would lead you to a West Key Number that closely matched the issue you were researching. Then we would use the Key Number to locate case decisions within the jurisdiction we were interested in finding. Then we would take the case cite from that index and go to the stacks (what libraries call rows and rows of shelves brimming with books filed with court decisions). There you would find the volume number and page number where the court decision started. If the court decision was similar to your case, and it seemed to favor your argument, yippee . . . well, not yet.

You had to go to another set of books called Shepherd's Citation Service. In a process called Shepardizing®, you would go through a bound volume that listed case citations (volume and page numbers of cases) followed by a list of other citations of cases that had discussed that case. There were abbreviations after each set of numbers indicating whether the court had merely discussed the case, agreed with it or, horror of horrors, overruled or reversed the decision in the case you had found. Mind you, we also had to check what was overruled, because it may have been part of the case you didn't care about, or the part essential to the argument we were preparing on our own case. Not only did we have to check the bound volume with this information, but we would have to update it with another soft covered book that had updates from the past couple of months and repeat the process, and then update with a third booklet with even more recent decisions.

After this process, we either had to go back to the cases and find a better or still valid case decision, or pray that we really had reviewed all of the proper books and completely Shepardized our case citation, thus rendering your legal citation "good law" upon which the Court could rely.

HELPFUL HACK

Because lawyers cannot feel 100% certain about anything, you can rephrase your questions to them to elicit more helpful responses. Instead of asking your lawyer "What should I do?" (which infers a single response), ask them "What is the best approach I can use here?" (which infers the existence of multiple options). This allows the lawyer to respond back to you with a range of options and the strengths and weaknesses of each. This will provide you with the information you need to make your own, informed decision. When there is a high level of risk associated with the course of action you take, ask for a more formal response from your lawyer, an opinion letter. An opinion letter can often be used as proof of your good faith conduct, even if later it is shown to have been mistaken.

Although much of this process is now computerized, if you pay WestLaw, LexisNexis, or a handful of other services, there's never any confidence that you really truly have found the proper case and that it has not been overturned or modified between the time you did your research and filed your brief, or when your motion is heard by the Court. I've had it happen when a new court decision came down literally the morning of my court hearing on precisely the issue I had before the Court. The judge already knew about it; I did not.

It's easier to invade a small country than to file a court document

In the United States you can order a pizza, buy a movie, or even obtain an arsenal of weapons with a few clicks of a keyboard or your smartphone. If you want to use the legal system, however, you must work within a near Stone Age technical system governed by the most complicated and overlapping set of rules, regulations, and conventions as to boggle even the most genius of meticulous legal minds. Advanced technology and the legal world have barely intersected.

Let's start with a little context. When someone has a dispute they need a court to resolve, the process is, in broad strokes, as follows. The party wanting relief (called a plaintiff) files a document with the court outlining what the facts are and why that entitled them to relief under the law (a complaint). The party on the other side of the dispute (defendant) is served with a copy of this document and gets a set amount of time to respond back, either acknowledging some or all of the points in the initial document or denying them (an answer). The complaint and answer outline the scope of the dispute.

There is a certain amount of time during which the parties exchange certain types of information and documents relating to the dispute (discovery), and then the case goes to a trial where each side makes their case, presents their evidence and witnesses, and then either a judge or a jury decide who wins.

Simple, right? Hardly. First of all, as you may have guessed from the section above, this process is a veritable manure-rich soil environment for nurturing disputes about which lawyers can argue. They argue about whether the complaint was properly served on the other party, whether it was filed in the right court, whether its contents are proper or sufficient, whether the case should proceed to declare that the defendant should win the case outright on the basis of the contents of the complaint, and, of course, there is no end to arguments over discovery, and how a trial will be run. There is literally no end.

I have seen cases where arguments over the contents and service of the complaint lasted over a year and cost the parties tens of thousands of dollars. I have also seen a lawyer file a motion challenging the contents of the complaint (a motion is a request to the court) without ever reading the complaint, and winning! He explained to me later that he needed more time to prepare an answer, and he was sure that statistically speaking there was probably something wrong with the third and fourth paragraph of any complaint.

HELPFUL HACK

When you are in a lawsuit, be engaged in the decision-making about motions that are filed. Always ask what the benefits are in filing, whether you will be giving up any important rights by not filing, and how much it will cost in time and money. Not all battles are worth fighting.

The procedural complexity goes far deeper than these "form over substance" battles. The actual act of filing documents with the court is remarkably antiquated and, dare I be so candid, stupidly designed.

Let me give you some examples. I was handling a lawsuit in the United States District Court for the Central District of California. This court handles a lot of important cases, large commercial disputes, civil rights cases, legal disputes between citizens of different states, lots of important stuff. You would think that a court handling such sophisticated subject matter would have sophisticated computer systems to handle all of the paperwork going back and forth and consistent treatment of documents. You would be wrong.

During the course of a lawsuit, there are likely to be hundreds or thousands of pages of documents filed with the court regarding the case, beginning with pleadings outlining the respective positions of the parties, and then many motions or requests to the court to decide parts of the case or argue over the exchange of information and documents (discovery) that occurs within the case. It used to be that whenever a side to the lawsuit had an issue to raise with the court they would prepare a document outlining what they wanted, what legal reason they believed supported their request, and what facts made their legal reason applicable. The party making the request would file the original document with the court (and maybe one copy), and send a copy to the other side in the lawsuit. For the ease of the court clerks, there were rules about how these documents needed to look and what information had to be contained in them, such as having the filer's name and contact information in the top left-hand corner, the case number prominently listed on the right side just above the name of the document, the parties' names on the left side. Some courts even required blue-backing, attaching a sheet of light blue cardstock to the back so it was easy to see where one document ended and the next began in the court's growing file of papers.

About 10 years ago, federal courts started using electronic filing systems. Yeah!!! Joining the rest of the world technology-wise. Very exciting, right? Well, not so much. Here are the steps you now need to follow to file a simple motion in this court.

First, you need to consult at least four or five sets of interlocking and overlapping rules and make sure you comply with every one. Consult the *Federal Rules of Civil Procedure* to make sure that the content of your motion or request to the court complies with permissible requests and permissible timeframes. Then consult and comply with the *Local Rules* for this particular United States District Court (each one is different) that have additional requirements to filings, including time and page limitations. This is not limited to font size and margin widths. Oh no, that would be too simple. Here's one example of the detailed procedures. If you are filing a motion relating to discovery (exchange of information between the parties in the case), you have to do the following:

┌─ HELPFUL HACK ─┐

Discovery disputes are one of the most expensive components of a lawsuit. Be proactive with your law firm to make sure discovery doesn't become a black hole for your money. Responses to written discovery requests should, whenever possible, follow the following format:

"Objection, [and then the lawyer can list all their 20 million objections to every nitpicky thing in the question]." Let the lawyer get that nitpickiness out of their system. Then, add the following: "Notwithstanding these objections, Responding Party responds as follows . . .." This format for responses will reduce the likelihood that the other attorney will complain about the response and file a motion to compel a better one, a process that, of course, takes more time and money. By just meaningfully answering questions in discovery, you reduce the need for dealing with these extra motions, resulting in direct monetary savings to you. There is no benefit in hiding the ball in the discovery process. If you have a bad case, it won't get any better through delay in disclosure of the facts.

1. Write a meet and confer letter to the other lawyer, explaining what you want and why.

2. Within 10 days after the letter, both lawyers must have a meet and confer conversation about what you want and why (and, of course, why they don't want to give it to you, and why). If both lawyers are located within the same county, the conference must take place at the

office of the moving party's lawyer's office, unless agreed otherwise. If they are not in the same county, then they can meet by telephone.

3. If the lawyers cannot agree (and let's face it, they almost never do), then they need to prepare a document together called a joint stipulation that contains both sides' positions on issues. The moving party is required to deliver a draft document, the other lawyer has 7 days to respond back, the information is merged together and then it has to be signed by the second lawyer and sent back by the end of the next business day so it can be filed with the court.

4. After the request and stipulation is filed with the court, the parties can file a supplemental document not later than 14 days prior to the hearing date.

Throughout these *Local Rules* are also page limitations, instructions on how to service (provide copies) of the documents required (personal, fax, email, etc.), and mandatory language to be placed here or there within the documents.

It takes about 15 minutes just to calendar all the deadlines, and then there is a huge likelihood that one of these deadlines conflicts with something else on your schedule. You could ask for a modification of the scheduling deadlines, but that process requires its own, different, set of procedures almost as daunting as the original one.

In addition, there are at least two other sets of rules to consult. Most of the individual judges have *Chamber Rules* governing how and when certain motions can be filed and how to schedule hearing dates. Some even place complete bans on contacting the judge's clerk by phone or email for any inquiries about anything. In most cases, there is both a Presiding Judge that makes major decisions, and a Magistrate Judge that makes other decisions. Both have their own chamber rules.

Finally, when it comes to the actual electronic filing of documents, there is another set of *Electronic Case Filing Rules* relating to technical requirements, format of documents (no embedded codes or hyperlinks, etc.), redaction of certain sensitive information, and also a list of certain documents that should not be electronically filed.

And after jumping through compliance with all of these interlocking rules, timeframes, technical requirements, page limits, mandatory language, conferences with other lawyers, you finally log onto the computer system that looks slightly more advanced than a DOS interface and upload your documents onto the computer system. Keep in mind that you need to categorize your document with the proper code from a list with often unclear terminology, codes that are not specifically tied with anything in the prior sets of rules you already reviewed. You are prompted throughout the process to not do this or that, don't use capital letters in any of the descriptive fields, don't attach this or that document, link this document to prior documents filed, etc. But finally, finally, you are through the mouse maze and hit the final approval button. Whew! Done. Electronic filing completed. Automatic email received confirming your filing and that it was also emailed to the other lawyer. You are done.

Hardly . . .

After electronically filing your request with the Court, you then need to send a proposed order in both .pdf and Word format to a specially-designated email address (different for each judge, of course). A proposed order repeats what you already asked for in the motion, but phrases it in terms of the judge having read your arguments and agreeing with you.

Done now?? No.

After all of that highly regulated and meticulous electronic filing, you then need to download and print out the entire document you just uploaded into the electronic system. After consulting the list of the meticulous different requirements for every judge regarding mandatory chambers copies, you arrange for a hard copy of the electronic filing to be personally delivered onto the judge's desk no later than noon the following day.

No kidding! The court website has an alphabetical list of every single judge and magistrate judge listing their specific requirements for chambers copies. Some just require a simple copy. Others demand attachment of a copy of the e-filing notice accompanying it. Others require insertion of tabs and marking of each document as "Chambers Copy" or "Court Copy" or "Mandatory Courtesy Copy." Some specify different delivery locations for different types of filings, some want blue-backing (some specifically do not want blue-backing), specific hole-punching, some specifically demand that the copies not be placed in envelopes, some want courtesy copies on CDs or flashdrives with hyperlinks (even though the electronic filing system rejects documents containing hyperlinks). One judge even has a separate list of types of documents for which he wants a courtesy copy, and another list for documents he does not want. Others want two copies of this document, and only one copy of another type of document. Not only are there a myriad of requirements from judge to judge, but some even threaten rejections of the documents, removal of hearing dates, or sanctions if these mandatory hard copies do not meet their nitpicky requirements.

The cost and time inefficiencies of all this hoop jumping burden falls directly on the clients. The lawyers bills for their time, their paralegal's time, and for reimbursement of all of the costs.

If the lawyer is reasonably organized and manages to finish the document by, say, noon on the day it is filed, she can print off the courtesy copy, put it in FedEx Priority Overnight and have it on the judge's desk by noon the next day. Priority overnight costs more than regular overnight, but still this is a better scenario than what usually happens.

Even using FedEx to transmit the paper courtesy copy will not meet most judge's requirements. The courtesy copy must be hand-deposited in a specific courtesy box outside of the judge's chambers, not the place where FedEx delivers packages. This often doesn't make much difference anyway, because of the timing of completion of briefs.

Lawyers are procrastinators and often don't complete a brief too far ahead of the midnight electronic filing deadline. More often than not, edits continue to be made throughout the day and evening, long enough to miss the FedEx deadline for overnight delivery. Thus, if the electronic filing is done at 11pm, the hard copy still has to be on the judge's desk by noon the following day—in 13 hours. There are two ways to make that happen. If the law office is close to the courthouse, they can send a runner over in the morning, or have an attorney service pick up and deliver it then. The approximate cost of that expedited service will cost about twice as much as FedEx would. But if the law office is not close enough to make that reasonably possible, they will have to transmit the copy of the electronically filed document to an attorney service located near to the courthouse, and the attorney service will print it out and personally deliver it to the judge's chambers. If it is a substantial document with lots of attached declarations and exhibits (as is common on even moderately complex cases), this can costs hundreds of additional dollars to simply file the request for relief with the court. These costs are billed out to the clients, sometimes at a markup, on top of the attorney fees for work on the substance of the document. Furthermore, all the time of paralegals spent on these details is also billed out to the clients, either directly (often at $90-$150/hr or more) or indirectly.

All of this meticulous detail for the sake of details has a much greater cost than financial, however. When lawyers have so many details that must be navigated to complete even the simplest of tasks, it materially affects their mental functions and makes it difficult for them to see the big picture of the client's legal matters and unable to see simple solutions to problems. It also makes them dreadfully fearful of missing details.

HELPFUL HACK

When your lawyer is working on writing and filing a motion, do not expect them to be calling you or responding to emails, other than if you are directly involved in drafting the document. Expect radio silence as they concentrate on these details. Any efforts you make to communicate about other aspects of the case will be billable time for which you get no benefit at all, so just wait until at least 24 hours after the motion is done and your lawyer has gotten a little sleep.

Daily dread of missing details

To a lawyer, every answer is fraught with the fear of making a mistake, minor or catastrophic, of failing to include every possible or potential concept, idea, or thought that may, could, or might be expressed heretofore or hereinafter that might be, in actuality, thought, or believed to be, either at the present time or at some prior or later date, whether or not such belief is rational, well-founded, or sensible, such that another lawyer, attorney, paralegal, or other legal professional, whether duly licensed or authorized or not, might, could, or would have the capacity to question, minimize, or undermine, in whole or in part, thereby rendering the answer to be, or upon reasonable or unreasonable objective or subjective belief, to be in error. . . .. (Sorry, I'm a lawyer, that's how our minds work). Simply put, the fear of missing details creates inefficiencies, even in writing documents.

Legal writing uses a number of different mechanisms to make "simple" less simple. Doublets and triplets of related words is one favorite mechanism—using several words to describe the same thing, but in slightly different ways. For example, "contract, agreement, or understanding" or "dispute, controversy, or claim." They all mean the same thing to any normal person, but lawyers are taught that there are fine distinctions between the words, so you might as well use all of them otherwise your professor, law school classmate, or opposing counsel will find a way to create an argument around your choice of language. Take a look at any contract you have (loan documents, credit card agreement, or similar documents). You will find them filled with doublets and triplets.

— HELPFUL HACK —

One way to keep legalese out of your business contracts is to create an initial draft yourself. Lawyers tend to copy documents from earlier client documents and hesitate to take words out because they may not be sure why they were there in the first place. This is why legal documents often look so antiquated; they are. If you first create your own document, then have your lawyer review it for missing details and confirming legal compliance, you are much more likely to get a legal document that reflects your business rather than the lawyer.

Another grammatical mechanism is the imprecise time reference, something I like to refer to as the "CYA time reference." Look at any lawsuit complaint and you will find at least one time or date reference prefaced with "on or about." "On or after" and "on or before" are other favorites, along with "in and around." Why don't they just say "On June 3, 2012, Jose and Martha entered into a contract"? Because there is a possibility, ever so slight, that in a dispute over said contract, it might be crucial whether the date was actually June 3rd or June 4th or even June 2nd. I mean, maybe the contract was signed by Jose at 11:57pm and by Mary at 12:01am. So instead of later being accused of being "wrong," the lawyer writes "on or about June 3rd" a description that courts have decided can include a timeframe as much as six months before or after the listed date.

Lawyers also like to use "whereas," "heretofore," "hereinafter," "arguendo," "aforementioned," and many other words that normal people don't use. Why? They make us sound impressive, educated, and generally snootier than the rest of you. (I'm not defending that practice, just noting it.) The other reason is because they spend so much time reading old court decisions or documents that include those words, it seeps into your pores.

> Lawyers use words normal people don't use to sound impressive, educated, and generally snootier.

To non-lawyers, who need some sense of certainty, of black and white, some manner of making decisions, this is frustrating beyond comprehension. I get that, but we lawyers can't really help ourselves. Notice how many pages it took me to explain why lawyers can't do "simple"? I had to drag my fingers away from the keyboard to keep it from being an even longer explanation.

Even though lawyers are solidly entrenched in complexity and ambiguity, they might be able to change their ways if there were any financial incentives to being simple and concise.

There are none.

FUELED BY FEAR AND ADRENALINE

Every human behavior can be explained by what precedes it,
but that does not excuse it.

-Gavin de Becker, *The Gift of Fear*

Understanding why lawyers act the way they do cannot be complete without looking at the very real physiological aspect of their day-to-day lives. They are haunted by pervasive fear and the accompanying fight-or-flight adrenaline rush that demands conquering of threats with perfect technique.

Every person has within them a primitive reaction to fear when faced with a threatening situation. Fear sets off a complex set of physiological reactions that allow a person to exert seemingly superhuman strength. This vitally important human survival mechanism, often referred to as the "fight or flight response" or "adrenaline rush," is great if you suddenly face a grizzly bear— it heightens the likelihood of your survival. Adrenaline rushes, however, can also be provoked by more innocuous threats.

In Gavin de Becker's remarkable book, *The Gift of Fear: Survival Signals That Protect Us from Violence*, he discusses the fact that people are almost as fearful of public speaking as they are of death. That fear, he explains, is deeply rooted in the same set of survival instincts. The fear of public speaking "is linked to the fear of being perceived as incompetent, which is linked to the fear of loss of employment, loss of home, loss of family, your ability to contribute to society, your value, in short, your identity and your life."[7]

Lawyers daily face that fear of incompetence, making every day a fight for professional survival. The first adrenaline rush of my legal career happened the first week of law school. University of Nebraska College of Law, Contracts class with Professor Denicola. I was sitting in a massive, tiered classroom with over 100 of my peers, intelligent, driven students that had competed with hundreds of other applicants to sit in the very seats they were now occupying. Although I was quite familiar and even comfortable with public speaking and music performance (and a touch of stage fright accompanying performance), I had no preparation for what happened next.

Let me explain how a law school classroom works. The "Socratic method" of teaching was created by Dean Langdell of Harvard Law School in the late nineteenth century and is still used in every law school in the country. Bestselling author, Scott Turow, in the book "One L" which recounts his own first year of law school in the 1970s describes the same method I was subjected to in the 1990s at the University of Nebraska School of Law. It's like this. The law professor will call on a student at random from the group of over 100 students. This student will be pelted with questions about the case being discussed. What was the issue in the case? How did the court rule? How is this case distinguishable from the last case we discussed? The student will be questioned until they get stymied and can answer no more. Lord help you if you fell asleep before reading the case the night before, or if you cannot distinguish the facts of this case from the 20 others you just read. Sometimes, with enough right answers, the professor will mercifully turn to another student to grill, but sometimes even knowing the student is unprepared, the professor will continue to come back to them to ask questions. The psychological import of this teaching paradigm is aptly described in Scott Turow's book, *One L.*[8]

> . . . [T]he Socratic method depends on a tacit license to violate a subtle rule of public behavior. When groups are too large for any semblance of intimacy, we usually think of them as being divided by role. The speaker speaks and, in the name of order, the audience listens— passive, anonymous, remote. <u>In using the Socratic method, professors are informing students that what would normally be a safe personal space is likely at any moment to be invaded.</u>

So there I was in Professor Denicola's class, my personal space had been invaded, I was the first student that year to be inducted into the Socratic method of teaching. I thought I was ready to be called on by the professor. I had read the assigned cases and prepared typewritten summaries for each case, outlining each relevant part of the case that I might be questioned on. I even printed it out in 14-pt typeface for ease of reading without squinting. But when Professor Denicola called on "Ms. Kramer" to give the summary of the first case in front of a hundred of my peers, those students with whom I would compete for the next three years for grades and thus job opportunities for the rest of my life, my mind went blank. I looked down at my notes and literally could not read them. They may as well have been written in hieroglyphics. I could see letters and words, but the part of my brain that processed words into audible sounds had literally shut down. I sat there frozen like some unfortunate deer in the headlights of a truck, unable to move to safety.

It wasn't until years later that I understood what happened to me that day. When the brain's amygdala fear center triggers, as mine most certainly had, it sets off a cascade of physiological reactions in the body. Heart rate and blood pressure increase, hormones including adrenaline and cortisol are released into the blood stream, all giving the body a boost in physical strength. This reallocation of body resources, however, means that some other functions have to be reduced. Sensory capabilities are limited, resulting in tunnel vision (narrowed scope of what your eyes see) and auditory exclusion (reduced reception of sounds). Fine motor skills disappear (forget trying to pick up pennies) and cortisol interferes with complex thinking (not the time to pull out a crossword puzzle). Sometimes the body just freezes, unable to react to its environment (sort of like a possum that plays dead when faced with an attacker).

The fear of looking like an idiot in front of all of those people in the high pressure environment of that law school classroom triggered my brain to react as though confronted with a grizzly bear. While I may have had the strength to pick up Professor Denicola and slam him against the wall, or sprint like an Olympic runner out the door, my complex thinking skills were temporarily gone, in my case, the ability to process the written word into spoken language.

> The fear of looking like an idiot triggered my brain to react as though confronted with a grizzly bear, shutting down my complex thinking skills.

The induced fear dynamic of the Socratic method can have an additional traumatic impact for women. A fellow student of Scott Turow confided in him about this.

> "When I get called on, I really think about rape. It's sudden. You're exposed. You can't move. You can't say no. And there's this man who's in control, telling you exactly what to do. Maybe that's melodramatic," she said, "but for me, a lot of the stuff in class shows up all kinds of male/female power relations that I've sort of been training myself to resent."[9]

While I wouldn't have analogized my personal experience in as strong a term are "rape," I will admit that this young woman's perceptions from the mid-70's at Harvard Law School weren't that much different from my experience at the University of Nebraska twenty years later. I was suddenly exposed to making a fool of myself in front of over 100 competitive classmates who would be judging my every utterance. I couldn't move. I couldn't speak. I couldn't decline to respond. I had only two options— learn to cope with the trauma, or quit.

I don't really remember what happened next that day in Professor Denicola's class. I suppose I was finally able to spit out some type of response sufficient to convince the professor to move on to another victim. Over time I developed coping mechanisms to deal with this fear reaction inherent in the legal teaching paradigm, but my body's visceral reaction to this fear remained and continued every time I appeared in court or at a deposition for the next 20 years of trial lawyer practice. My primary coping mechanism was to *act* as though I have no fear; I run towards the grizzly bear, run into the burning building, take on any lawyer in court.

> [C]lassroom terror has been a fixed aspect of legal
> education for at least a century. But the risk, the
> ultimate risk, of allowing students to make their first
> acquaintance with the law in such an atmosphere,
> in that state of hopeless fright, is that they will come
> away with a tacit but ineradicable impression that it is
> somehow characteristically "legal" to be heartless, to be
> brutal, and will carry that attitude with them into the
> execution of their professional tasks.[10]

This mode of interaction between professor and student continues on in courtrooms. Lawyers are frequently mocked, ridiculed, and demeaned by judges or sanctioned thousands of dollars because the judge was in a bad mood. Lawyers can do nothing but say "thank you, Your Honor" and take it. Unsurprisingly, the lawyers then take out this pent up frustration on each other and sometimes their clients.

What kind of fool would subject themselves to that situation over and over again? Competitive, driven, crazy people. The only way you can cope with the adrenaline rush is to embrace it, channel it, and use it to be the fierce, take-no-prisoners litigator that clients both love and revile. You have to become an adrenaline addict and so does every other lawyer with whom you interact. To be a trial lawyer, you have to become tough and heartless and intense. You have to become a mercenary (and sometimes also an alcoholic or a drug addict.)

If you think that your lawyer is sometimes not listening to you or not seeing evidence right in front of their faces, your observations may be right on the money, especially during court cases. Over and over again I hear clients say "I told my lawyer X, Y and Z at the last hearing and now they act as though they never heard me say it" or "He had the document he needed right in front of him; what is he, blind?" Chances are the lawyer is not "acting." It is quite possible they did not hear what you said and did not see the document to which you are referring. Being in court induces the fight or flight response to one degree or another, and that includes auditory exclusion (they really aren't hearing what you say) and tunnel vision (they can't see things right in front of them). Trial lawyers almost always have a second person sitting next to them in court for the sole purpose of handing them documents or even their pen when needed, because they cannot find anything on their own counsel table while they are in the midst of trial. You will also find that lawyers who spend time in court almost universally will feel very tired an hour or two after court, some even having a routine of a nap after court hearings. This is because as soon as the adrenaline rush starts to dissipate, their bodies no longer have adrenaline to act as a stimulant to overcome their endless fatigue from too many long hours working.

HELPFUL HACK

Immediately before and after court appearances is the worst time to have a substantive discussion with your lawyer about anything other than the hearing itself. It will be wasted billable time because the lawyer will be so focused on the task at hand that he or she won't remember anything you say and will not be in a state that allows for complex thinking.

BECAUSE DUELS
ARE ILLEGAL

"Lawyers confuse being zealous with being crazy."

- Anonymous Attorney

The point in having a court system and jury trials to resolve disputes is to avoid bloodshed in the streets. It used to be that if two gentlemen in early America had a dispute, one would challenge the other to a duel; that would quickly and easily resolve the dispute. A duel requires two offended parties, each with a second person present, I suppose to call a doctor or haul off the body, depending on the aim of the parties. The great thing about duels was that they were quick, cheap, and easily and permanently resolved disputes. However, dueling is now illegal, so now we are left with the court system. Unfortunately, I suspect that many litigants would prefer the risk of getting shot to the hell of a lawsuit.

Over the centuries, predecessor models to judicial (court) resolution of disputes had two primary modes— trial by ordeal (common to many cultures worldwide) and trial by combat (primarily of Germanic origin).

Trials by combat included dueling, fencing, and other types of combat. Sometimes it was the witnesses, not the litigants, who engaged in combat. Women over a certain age, minors, and the infirm could get a jury trial. Fighting continued until one party was dead or disabled, thus determining victor and vanquished. Sometimes another person (a precursor to today's litigation attorneys) would make logistical arrangements for the combat, including trying to resolve the dispute short of risking their clients' life or limb.

Trial by ordeal has more ancient and more widespread history. Trial by ordeal consists of subjecting the accused to some type of unpleasant, sometimes potentially deadly, experience. Survival equated with innocence. Unlike trials by combat, trial by ordeal often had a direct connection to religious beliefs, namely that God would intervene to protect an innocent person and perform a miracle. Ironically, in early America during the infamous witch-hunts, the concept of trial by ordeal was reversed. For example, if an accused witch was thrown in the river with a rock tied around them, if they sank and drowned, they were considered innocent, but if they did not drown, that was taken as evidence of guilt.

The current American judicial system seems to have incorporated some of the worst parts of both trial by combat and trial by ordeal. Upon close analysis, its model is remarkably similar to methods of warfare used in World War I and World War II. Sometimes opposing parties fought each other from opposing trenches in long-drawn out land wars, other times there were blitzkrieg attacks and atomic bombs, but the goal of both was to cause so much destruction and death that eventually one side could declare victory over the other. The difference between a simple trial by combat and a world war is really only a matter of degree, the volume of resources allocated to the fight, and the willingness to inflict widespread carnage on both combatants and civilians around them. With military and civilian casualties numbering over 17 million as a result of World War I, and over 60 million as a result of World War II, it is not much of a leap to suggest that perhaps we should seek out a different model for conflict resolution within our civilian justice system.

The current American judicial system seems to have incorporated some of the worst parts of both trial by combat and trial by ordeal.

Civil lawsuits begin with the equivalent of throwing down a gauntlet signaling an invitation to a duel, otherwise known as the demand letter. This letter is a threat. Whether it's one page long or 50 pages, the message is simple—do what I am demanding or I will drag you to court.

Demand letters are very effective weapons of intimidation. It is similar to the person who brings a gun to the workplace and waves it around threatening to shoot if he doesn't get his job back. That is intimidating. Not usually effective for any other purpose, though.

A few years ago I took a self-defense class. We started by sitting in a circle passing around a training knife and gun. In turn we each introduced ourselves and, as we held the two weapons in our hands, explained which one we feared more and why. As we went around the circle, listening to the students' worst fears, I noticed that the fears had little to do with reality. Most students had never been directly threatened with either of the weapons, but all had fears connected with them. The gun seemed more threatening or scary to most; to me it was the knife. Why? Because I knew that statistically people with guns are a lot less accurate shots than you would think, even at close range, and furthermore, you only needed to be outside of the trajectory of a bullet to avoid injury. A knife, on the other hand, could cause immense damage without much precision.

I have to wonder how my classmates would have reacted to having a third threatening object in their hands— a summons and complaint commencing a lawsuit. In some ways, that is even more threatening than knives or guns. Lawsuits can cause immense damage without precision and despite eventual outcome.

Most weapon-wielding assailants don't want to use their weapon. In fact, I understand from experts that, statistically, if the weapon is not used within the first few seconds of an encounter, chances are it won't be used at all. The person holding a gun or a knife simply wants to intimidate their victim into compliance.

Threats of filing a lawsuit are used in exactly the same way as a gun or knife. The person making the threat usually doesn't really want to go to court, they just want to intimidate the recipient of the demand letter to do what they are being asked to do. The demand letter is very, very effective at inducing terror in recipients, however, it is very, very ineffective at getting what the person sending it really wants.

One of the most frequent requests I have heard over the years is the "Can you just send _____ a letter on your letterhead? That ought to scare them into (refunding my money, or whatever)." This is usually accompanied by the explanation "I don't want to go to court. If they see the letter from a lawyer, they'll know I'm serious." For many years, I would naively accommodate these requests. After many years of doing this, and matters promptly deteriorating shortly thereafter, I had to do some analysis, some introspection at the dynamic, and I now respectfully decline most such requests.

Here's the thing. What I'm being asked to do is to intimidate the other person. Would I agree if they asked me to put a gun to someone's head? Absolutely not. No question. So why would I acquiesce to this request for me to threaten another person with a different weapon?

The requesting person thinks that this intimidation will make the other side "come to their senses" and do what the other person wants.

The truth is this rarely works anyway. I used to think it didn't work because I was often bluffing, but there were other reasons too.

Early in my legal career I contemplated buying a handgun. I was a single woman living by myself, working as a criminal prosecutor in one county, and criminal defense attorney in another. Although my criminal defense clients had every motivation to kiss up to me and treat me well, I occasionally made them mad and even if they were incarcerated, they had friends who weren't. I mentioned my intention to a friend who was a law enforcement officer and combat vet. He looked me straight in the eye and asked "Are you willing to take the life of another person? If you aren't, you should not get a gun."

I chose not to get a gun because I wasn't sure if I could take the life of another person, at least not with a gun. It had been traumatic enough when another person had died after running a red light and colliding with my car. I did, however, keep a baseball bat in my entry closet thereafter. I was pretty confident I was willing to swing a bat in self-defense at a home intruder and cause enough damage to give me a chance to call the police.

After that, I took the same approach with demand letters. If a client asked me to send such a letter, I made them commit to following through with filing a lawsuit if the demand letter did not work.

Here's the other problem with demand letters. Because threatening a lawsuit is tantamount to putting a gun to someone else's head, such an action, through pure biological processes, is not likely to bring someone to their senses, certainly not to have them look at a problem logically. A victim at gunpoint is not thinking about bullet trajectories or statistics of accuracy of aim. It feels like their very life is at stake, and their brain shifts from its calm, analytical high brain into its primate, low brain, reactive survival response, even in response to the slightest bit of perceived threat. They are more likely primed to defend themselves by any means necessary (or at any price), rather than either agreeing to the demands made or to work cooperatively towards some other resolution. This creates a perfect time for a defense attorney to lock in a fee agreement for spending an unspecified number of hours and costs in order to defend the case.

> ## ┌─ HELPFUL HACK ─
>
> If you are on the receiving end of a demand letter, no matter how nasty or threatening, take some deep breaths and realize that it is only as threatening as you allow it to be. The other side is feeling desperate, feeling out of options to get what they want in any other way. Don't react in anger. Cool down. Then give them an option that does not involve a lawsuit. They will probably take it.

There is also another problem, a biological reaction within the body of the sender of a demand letter (the person pointing the weapon at a victim). Remember the self-defense class? At one point in the class we were practicing disarming an assailant. I felt the adrenal rush when I was the mock victim with a training weapon against my throat, but when I was playing the assailant, oh wow, the adrenal rush was even more intense. That isn't healthy, but it's a real part of litigation threats. For both the sending attorney and the client, it engages their primitive brains that want to win, want to defeat an opponent, the non-rational brain. It is also the perfect time for an attorney to get a fee agreement signed that is either a gamble on the outcome of the battle (contingency agreement) or an unspecified amount of time to deal with the opposing party (an hourly agreement).

An unsuccessful demand letter means there is no resolution between the parties with a dispute. The person initiating the process demands "justice," meaning something more like a Shakespearean "pound of flesh." The other person feels offended and frightened about what will come next, and also demands "justice," meaning something more like retaliation. This starts the chain reaction of a descent into hell that is commonly known as the civil lawsuit.

It only takes a couple of hundred dollars to file a complaint in a local courthouse, an entry ticket to making the other side expend time and money and emotional energy to defend. Enter the lawyers. Trained mercenaries, not diplomats.

Even the most battle-worn litigator can manage at least one or two civil telephone conversations, but you would never, ever consider sending a litigator to negotiate a cease-fire. There's a point when you realize the other side isn't going to back down. That is when the claws and fangs come out and the mercenary nature kicks in. After all, lawyers are hired to "win," not hired to "be nice" to the other side.

Unfortunately, the structure of the legal system is set up to prolong and increase the nastiness between both sides and present opportunities for private bludgeoning, over and over and over again. The fighting is stretched out over the course of a year or more so the parties and attorneys have some rest breaks in the middle to regain their fighting strength.

It's worthy of mentioning here that the most skilled mediator I ever encountered specifically denied parties and counsel rest breaks in the middle of settlement negotiations, even denying them lunch breaks. He would send them downstairs to grab a snack or sandwich, but they had to bring their food back upstairs to eat while the negotiations continued. By late afternoon everyone was too tired to keep fighting, and resolution was finally reached.

Now, before you completely blame either the lawyers or the system entirely, as much as people complain about lawyers arguing too much, they wouldn't hire lawyers that didn't vigorously argue with the other side. In fact, if you, as an attorney, don't vigorously argue and speak ill of the other side, your client may suggest that perhaps you are colluding with the other side or not doing your job properly. Believe it or not, I have actually received complaints from clients when my monthly bills were too low, reflecting, they thought, insufficient vigor on their behalf in the case.

Interpersonal interactions can be responded to anywhere on a gradation between passive and aggressive. On one end of the spectrum is passive. Imagine the skinny kid (we'll call him Sheldon) on the playground being confronted by the playground bully (we'll call him Billy Bob). Sheldon stands with shoulders hunched, eyes down, body partially turned away, and in a high pitched, quiet voice says "please don't hurt me." This is extreme passive behavior. Contrast the body language of Billy Bob, chest out, mean frown, gruff, loud voice, maybe pointing a finger or threatening with a fist. He represents the other end of the spectrum, aggressive. Neither extreme is a good way to go through life. React to others with passivity and you'll lose your lunch money every day. Be an aggressive bully, and you'll end up in the principal's office and later in jail.

Now imagine that you have to pick one of those two people to represent your interests, to fight for justice on your behalf. Are you going to pick Sheldon who is the sweetest and smartest kid, or Billy Bob who gets the job done? You'll say nasty things about Billy Bob behind his back, say what an insensitive brute he is and a lousy human being, but you will never, not in a million years, pick Sheldon to stand up for you when he has shown he doesn't even know how to stand up for himself.

So, you have two people who in the old days would have settled their dispute with a duel, now select the most aggressive lawyers they can find to "fight for their rights" in court.

The procedural framework of civil lawsuits is an ongoing series of procedural disputes directed towards an eventual trial of the real, underlying dispute. To get to the real dispute, you can expect battles over everything. A lawsuit starts out with a formal Complaint being personally served on the defendant, a document outlining why the plaintiff thinks the law and facts entitle them to some relief against the defendant. This first salvo raises all sorts of potential issues for lawyers to argue about. Was the document properly served (in the right format, by the right person, in the right place)? Does the chosen court have authority to decide the dispute (Can it require the defendant to submit to its decision)? Is this court authorized to review this type of case?) Is the complaint sufficient in its description of the facts and legal basis such that, if all true, would entitle the plaintiff to what he's asking for?

> Two people who in the old days would have settled their dispute with a duel, now select the most aggressive lawyers they can find to "fight for their rights" in court.

These types of questions formed the basis of a law student's first year class on civil procedure. Students "issue spot" and learn how to identify every potential problem. Similarly, the attorney hired by the defendant will be sure to see all of these potential challenges and will be happy to fight out any or all of these issues. Lawyers become particularly good at this when they get paid by the hour to identify issues and draft documents challenging every nitpicky thing they can think of. Law students only stop issue spotting when they run out of time at the end of an exam; there are no points for finishing early. Is it little wonder then that lawyers don't know when or how to stop fighting?

Then there are the mediations or settlement conferences, supposedly designed to create a quick end to lawsuits. Various courts schedule these alternative dispute resolution procedures at different steps in the case. My favorite wasteful use of time is federal court's Early Neutral Evaluation conference. On paper, having a conference with a judge early on, to review the scope of the case, the relative positions of the parties, and try to resolve the case, sounds like a good idea. However, it does not take into account human nature and lawyer nature.

Within the first few months of a lawsuit, the parties are all amped up for battle. The plaintiff's attorney has filed a complaint that not only paints the defendant as a bad actor, but requests a best-case scenario outcome for the plaintiff. The defendant is grossly offended (and it's amazing how even corporations who deal with litigation all the time seem to have officers personally offended at being sued). Now you bring each of these parties, along with their hired gun lawyers, to a first meeting with the judge, opposing counsel, and the opposing party. Keep in mind that all of these people may not have ever met before, clients are in an unfamiliar environment, and everybody is on heightened alert physiologically. Everyone but the judge is highly adrenalized. The lawyers are comparing themselves, how smart they are, how well spoken, how casually dismissive of the other side. The lawyers are sure their clients are also comparing them, much like an audience viewing boxers about to go into the ring.

Now can you picture this group of people being ready to roll up their sleeves and work hard to hammer out a compromise? Absolutely not! Would you expect boxers to join hands and sing "Kumbaya" together before stepping into the ring? It's ludicrous.

Although I have seen judges give a solid try to settle cases at this level, it is almost never successful. Even they acknowledge openly that the parties need to litigate a bit (i.e. beat up on each other through paperwork and rack up thousands of dollars in attorney fees) before they will be willing to even entertain the possibility of settlement.

HELPFUL HACK

Never forget that disputes must eventually be resolved, in one way or another. Create a reminder sheet for yourself that describes the dispute and what your position and the other person's position is. Then make weekly or monthly notations showing how much money and time you have spent, and what shift in movement has been made by either side. The reason for this documentation is to help you get out of the emotion of the dispute and back to practicalities. You'll soon learn that being inflexible is just costing you a lot of money and time.

Keep in mind, too, that each side has prepared a settlement brief, sometimes confidential for only the settlement judge to see, sometimes exchanged with the other side. The plaintiff's brief will contain monetary demands grossly exceeding any estimate of potential liability which defendant may have made, and the defendant's brief will contain something just as foolish the other way, suggesting that dismissal and an apology is the only way to resolve this matter. You may think I am overstating the matter; I am not. Here is the final paragraph of a mediation brief I once received just hours prior to the scheduled time for the parties to meet together to discuss settling the case.

In order to settle Ms. Brown[1]'s case, Ms. Brown would be required to reimburse all defense attorneys' fees to date, engage in anger management courses and issue a letter of apology to all defendants. Without such consideration from Ms. Brown, defendants are prepared to defend this case at trial.

---

[1] Not the client's real name

It shouldn't take a genius to figure out that there was no possible way for any mediator, however skilled, to bring the parties to a cooperative settlement agreement with that last minute attack. One side is demanding things they could not get even if they won the case at trial. It was an absurd position designed to anger Ms. Brown and extend the conflict, not work towards resolution. The conflict continued on for years after that.

This dynamic of goading the other side was beautifully illustrated in a social science experiment conducted by researchers at the University of Michigan in the early 1990s. Psychologists Dov Cohen and Richard Nisbett were studying what they called the "culture of honor," a cultural legacy borne out of the survival needs of herdsmen versus that of farmers. Farming cultures require community cooperation to survive, and no one interaction between two people is likely to completely destroy one's livelihood. Herdsmen, however, lived under constant threat of their herds, and their very means of survival, being taken away. Aggression, even at the slightest challenge, is required to maintain the necessary reputation to dissuade others who might otherwise take away his livelihood. This, in a nutshell, is a "culture of honor." It also seems to correlate with the concept of trial by combat discussed earlier.

Cohen and Nisbett wanted to test whether this culture of honor legacy continued from generation to generation even though successive generations were no longer herdsmen. To test their hypothesis they gathered a group of young men and insulted them, then tested their reactions. Each test participant was sent down a hallway to deliver a questionnaire. For the control group, nothing else happened. For the others, however, they had an apparent bystander be in the narrow hallway, calling the test subject an "asshole" as they walked past. They took measurements of how angry the subjects were through visible cues on their faces, firmness of handshake grip, as well as levels of testosterone and cortisol. They also had each subject provide a conclusion to a short story. The short story was about some guy making a pass at their girlfriend at a party. There were distinct differences in how they responded to being insulted. Some laughed it off, with unchanged handshakes, lowered cortisol levels, and non-violent conclusions to the stories. For others, the response was very angry, with jumps in testosterone and cortisol, firmer handshakes, and ending the story being all over the guy who was hitting on the girlfriend.

In another exercise, they did a game of chicken, sending a big, bouncer type guy down the narrow hall and measured the distance at which the test subject would move out of the way. For some, having been insulted made no difference in the distance, for others, the insult made a huge difference. Some subjects who had been very deferential before the insult, got right up close after being insulted, seven feet closer, as a matter of fact.

While Cohen and Nisbett concluded that the difference between test subjects was their heritage, Southerners vs. Northerners, I saw something different. I saw the art of manipulating adrenal response levels in other people.

Several years ago I stumbled across a unique self-defense training program called FAST Defense. This training delves into the murky world of the body's fight or flight response in our bodies[11]. FAST Defense is asymmetrical, scenario-based adrenal stress training which, in simpler terms, involves a simulated attack by a stranger. It is not martial arts with stylized and complicated series of motions; it is down and dirty, gotta-save-your-life stuff. It's also about recognizing your own body's reaction to the rush of adrenaline when provoked by fear or insult, and learning to maintain the appropriate balance of response. Often a potential physical conflict can be de-escalated verbally, but if it becomes physical you need to be able to harness the power of your adrenal response to maximize your response. Maintaining a middle ground seems to be the hardest task.

Compare Cohen and Nisbett's testing scenario with that of a FAST Defense training scenario.

> For scenario-based training to work, there must be someone to play the role of a credible bad guy. We call this guy the woofer. Just like a dog trying to intimidate its victim by going "woof woof," the woofer's objective is to elicit an adrenal response in the student through a barrage of verbal assaults, foul language, and innuendo.[12]

Having now both participated in and coaching many FAST classes, I can tell you that a skilled woofer can invoke a full-on adrenal response with only a few words or even through body language alone. Woofing is a day-to-day pastime for litigation lawyers.

⌐ HELPFUL HACK ¬

What are your trigger words? What can someone else say that gets your blood boiling? These are the words that can deprive you of your ability to think logically about your legal problems and solutions. Do not make decisions when someone has just triggered those things for you. Wait until the next day or until you have had an opportunity to calm down.

I discovered my written "woofing skills" long before I ever heard of FAST Defense. After practicing law for several years, I was handling insurance defense cases—car accidents and such. In some respects, it was pretty boring law. One of my cases should have been the least emotional of all lawsuit types—a subrogation case where one insurance company sues another to reimburse for a payout they made for a car accident. Completely disconnected from the people involved in the accident, it is just about dollars and cents. In this case, it only involved around $10,000, pennies in terms of insurance companies. Opposing counsel, a woman, was somewhat unpleasant to deal with, but we managed to get the case through the necessary steps to trial. Trial lasted an hour or two; she won, yay her. That's when it started to get interesting.

My client insurance company now was obliged to write an insubstantial-sized check to her client insurance company. My client needed a tax ID number for tax reporting of the payment. Standard, necessary stuff, requested in every case. Opposing counsel refused. For the next six months, we exchanged letters, her demanding the check, me saying I was happy to turn over the check if she just provided the tax ID number. I discovered that if I used any of a short list of words in my letters (I believe they included "ridiculous," "incompetent," and "absurd"), she would go, pardon my language, bat-crap crazy! It was unreal. Things got to the point that when I called her office to try to talk through the impasse, her secretary said she was refusing to talk with me. Mind you, I stood ready, willing and able to send the check and she was refusing to talk to me. Woofer— 1; victim— 0.

The dark confession I must make is that I enjoyed making her angry. With just a few words, devoid of even body language, I controlled her to her own detriment. I had never knowingly done that before and I shouldn't have enjoyed it so much. It was then that I started fearing that being a lawyer was eroding my humanity.

This was not an anomaly in the legal world. Woofing is a favorite lawyer pastime, in writing or in person. I recently had an older, male attorney actually leap towards me, putting his face within inches of my face trying to intimidate me. I've got to say, though, that if I hadn't already been in years of "recovery" from over-adrenalized reactions, he would have been in a world of hurt. I had a pen in my hand that would have gone nicely into his eyes, and due to our relative body positions, I was teed up for a clear shot at kicking him squarely in the groin. He really owes the self-control tenet of taekwondo and skilled FAST Defense instructors for his escape from a trip to the hospital that day.

HELPFUL HACK

Minimize the emotional impact of your lawsuit on the rest of your life by setting aside specific times to review information from your lawyer. If you read emails throughout the day from your lawyer where they have forwarded you insulting communications from the other side, it will rile you up and completely interfere with your ability to do anything else. Set up a plan, and notify your lawyer in advance, to look at incoming communications on case developments during specific windows of time. For example, ask your lawyer to put URGENT in all email communications that require prompt response from you, but otherwise you will consider all of the emails as something you will review within a few days.

Had this lawyer tried that stunt on another day, I might not have been able to summon up that self-control. After you have been verbally attacked and harassed on an ongoing basis in your job, there is a certain point where your adrenal stress state is constantly maintained and you cannot get it down to a restful level. At this point, you will react not only to the slightest provocation, but even the possibility of a provocation. This woofing behavior becomes even more pronounced in depositions, against those poor unfortunate souls who are parties or witnesses and are required to sit and be questioned endlessly by lawyers. Depositions are frequently veritable chambers of horror where interrogation under bright lights and cameras inflict terrible harm. Why more depositions do not end in physical violence, I do not know.

> After you have been verbally attacked and harassed on an ongoing basis, you will react to even the possibility of a provocation.

This over-heightened state of adrenaline was never more evident than during my first experience with 48 Hours of Adrenaline, a weekend training event run by FAST Defense. I knew enough about the training methods at that point to know that throughout the weekend I would face numerous mock attacks that I would be forced to defend. My mind and body didn't bother waiting for an actual attack to happen though.

Within the first hour of the weekend we were doing a simple drill that was not intended to involve any physical contact at all with the instructor. This drill was about keeping distance, gauging whether the person approaching me was any threat, and verbally de-escalating any threat there might be. There I stood about 15 feet away from a good looking Air Force guy, precisely the type of guy whose attention I would want if I weren't married, and he said "You have beautiful eyes." I felt my brain processing the situation. How far away was he? Plenty far that he was no threat. What was his body language? Relaxed, not threatening. Did he have a weapon in his hand? No. What was the content and tone of his words? The words could simply be a compliment, and there was nothing about the tone that was offensive or disrespectful, much less threatening. The appropriate response would have been to smile, say thank you, and just keep on walking. That's not what I did, though.

"BACK OFF!!!!! BACK OFF!!!!" I heard myself screaming at him. Oh, how similar that was to every lawsuit I ever handled. I knew the interaction would become nasty at some point—it always did—so why wait to react with fury?

The feeling of the adrenaline rushing inside my body is identical, whether an instructor is woofing me, I am cross-examining a witness, or I am arguing with opposing counsel. It was a little scary when I realized the same force within me that was tapped to defend against a mugger or rapist was what I used every day as a lawyer. My instinctive desire during my first FAST Defense class to run across the room and put my hands around the throat of the woofer who was taunting me was identical to the desire to wring the neck of a disrespectful lawyer on the other side of the table at a rancorous deposition.

> The same force within me that would defend me against a mugger or rapist is what I use every day as a lawyer.

LITIGATION IS A BLOOD SPORT

"I am tired and sick of war. Its glory is all moonshine. It is only those who have neither fired a shot nor heard the shrieks and groans of the wounded who cry aloud for blood, for vengeance, for desolation. War is hell."

-William Tecumseh Sherman

Dan[2] sat across the table from me at the local coffee shop. I didn't know him well, I just knew he was a successful business man, an older gentleman active with his family and at his local Jewish center, and that he had an experience from his past that he wanted to share with me when he found out I was writing this book. After chatting a bit, I pressed him for the story, of what exactly had happened all those years ago that he had promised to share with me.

---

[2] not his real name

His memory was detailed. The day when a SWAT team descended upon his suburban home and arrested him in a case of tragic, but avoidable, mistaken identity, was permanently etched in his memory. The mistake was acknowledged fairly promptly, and he was not detained in jail for long. He eventually learned that the authorities knew of the mistaken identification before they executed the raid, but proceeded to arrest him anyway.

A lawsuit was filed to address the unjust actions taken against him, and after four years, justice was finally done and the case was over. By that time the defense lawyers had deposed him for more time than he had been in custody. They had deposed his wife, his children, their nanny. It had been endless, the pressure intense, and eventually cost him his marriage. But he wasn't telling me everything still; I could sense it. I waited, and finally it came out.

"Do lawyers in depositions say things to try to upset you, to try to make you react in anger?" he asked.

I grimaced. "Yes," I admitted and knew I had been guilty of that many, many times, and so was practically every lawyer who has ever done a deposition. I could see a steely look come into his eyes, tenseness in his body, and knew he was reliving a moment in his deposition. "What did they ask you?" I asked.

"They asked me how I felt about the Holocaust."

My jaw dropped in horror. Even I would never stoop that low—at least I hoped I wouldn't. Here was a man who by surname and activities was obviously of Jewish descent, and by age, old enough to have a deep visceral reaction to discussions of mass genocide of Jews during the Holocaust. Indeed, it was entirely likely that he had lost family members in one of the many death camps. Any sense of human decency would demand the upmost care in even bridging the topic of the Holocaust with this man, especially a stranger.

Dan had been the victim of one injustice—a knowingly wrongful arrest by the police—but in order to "get justice" he had to surrender to the interrogation of a hateful attorney who purposely triggered painful emotions by asking a question that had nothing to do with the case.

I wish Dan's story was atypical. I wish it was just a random incident of some insensitive attorney, but it isn't. It is part of what we as lawyers do, sometimes being a bit harsh in order to ferret out the truth (or at least that is what we tell ourselves), but soon it loses even the pretense of noble purpose. We want to "win." We want to force our view of a case onto others.

> I deal with life or death situations sometimes. And lawyers get hired to come in and question my clinical decisions when they have no clue what kind of traumas I'm correcting…and they try and nail me to the wall because of a technicality. There are NO absolutes in the [operating room]…so how can they try and pass judgment on what I do?"
>
> – A trauma surgeon

We pass judgment because that is what we have been hired to do. We become bullies because we can, and because, as painful as it is for me to admit this to myself, we come to like it. We begin to enjoy the hunt, begin to like the taste of blood. For us as litigators, we are engaged in a modern version of trial by combat, and the litigants are being subjected to trial by ordeal.

HELPFUL HACK

You can save thousands of dollars in litigation costs by reigning in your attorney on depositions. Don't approve the costs unless the attorney explains exactly what information they are trying to get from the deposition and why they cannot get it through a more inexpensive method.

When I was a child, bullying was never discussed beyond the useless platitude of "sticks and stones can break my bones, but words will never hurt me." That was, and is, a blatant falsehood. Words hurt far more than sticks and stones ever can.

Bullying between kids at school was a rampant problem on every playground and in every lunch room even when I was a kid. Usually I was able to avoid the fray and, in fact, I went out of my way to avoid it. Between my height and having a very protective big brother, I was only rarely a victim of bullying, but I didn't escape it entirely. I remember one instance on the school bus when an older girl sat next to me and then started shoving me up against the window followed by five or six friends piling on top of me. That happened in first grade, yet its memory has never left me. There were also plenty of the verbal taunts and bullying that girls are especially known for. One girl in junior high and high school was especially mean and I used to pray for the bus driver to drive faster to get to her stop so I could continue the ride home in peace.

Having been raised in a fundamentalist Christian home, I was schooled in the reaction of "turning the other cheek" and was never taught to stand up for myself. In fact, I was explicitly forbidden from fighting back. I was raised to be a victim. While that is a problem in itself (in terms of my personal safety), it had a secondary, far more damaging effect. I never realized that I had the capacity of being a bully. Not only did I have the capacity (as all people do, no matter how meek and mild they may appear), but every time I was bullied it fueled a deep anger deep inside my soul that eventually would have to be expressed somewhere. Being a trial lawyer gave me the opportunity, though I didn't realize it until many years later.

Although it is the party or witness being questioned who takes the worst of the abuse in a deposition setting, the effects of the trauma also spread to the lawyers. I've sat next to clients being harassed and harangued by opposing counsel, knowing there was little I could do to stop it. Sometimes I ended the deposition instead of allowing the harassment to continue and, though my client got a brief respite, the judge soon ordered her to return to be deposed again, and for as long as the opposing counsel wanted. The deposition questioning continued for another three days. I'm not ashamed to admit that, after the first day, my adrenal system (fighting to protect my client) was shot. I had to ask a colleague to cover the remaining deposition sessions. I just couldn't sit by and watch what was happening anymore. For the next year, I refused to enter a deposition room.

HELPFUL HACK

Videotaping of depositions is usually allowed, but not required, and at least doubles the expense. Additional expenses are incurred later for editing the video for use at trial. If your lawyer proposes incurring this cost, make sure there is a specific reason other than being able to intimidate the witness with a bunch of bright lights.

Even outside of the deposition room, the abuse and nonsense continue. Craziness is contagious. There comes a point when the adversarial nature of litigation takes away your ability to be rational on any level. If you were able to stand back as a disinterested third party and view your communications, you would realize how crazy they are, but because you are neck deep in crazy, you can't even see it.

It should have been a simple divorce case[3]. The parties, with the aid of their attorneys, should have been able to negotiate the details of the break-up of a 25+ year marriage. There were high emotions

---

[3] Some of the details have been changed to protect the identity of the parties involved.

on both sides, but that is not unusual. There were accusations of domestic abuse, not unusual either. The lawyers should have acted as buffers between the disputing sides, but nothing of the sort happened here. One lawyer decided to take it upon himself to heap abusive conduct and threats on both the spouse and the spouse's attorney. Early in the case, a voicemail message was left for the attorney:

> You know, you need to get this battle ax [your client] under control before somebody shoots her which [chuckles] probably is the best thing for society, although I'm not going to recommend it to anybody. But she's a bitch on wheels and I'm sorry you are still stuck in this case, but that's your choice. You can call if you have any disagreement with this. Get your client under control or I'll drag her into court.

I entered the case several years into this saga. I resolved to myself, my client, and opposing counsel, to de-escalate the nastiness. Here's a quote from one of my first letters to this attorney.

> Let me say just briefly that I understand that you and [my client] have had disagreements over time. Any such issues need to be set aside so we can all properly and professional[ly] do our jobs to resolve this matter.

My plea for professionalism fell on deaf ears. Things started to deteriorate in a hurry. In response to my request for an expected check, opposing counsel responded with a refusal and volley of nasty comments about my client. Naively thinking I could still get the professionalism back on track, I responded like this.

> I understand that you and [my client] have had many misunderstandings in the past, but that is no reason to ignore emails or delay actions. Let's just all take a few deep breaths and then get our work done professionally and promptly, and then there will be no further need for either of you to annoy each other anymore.

I then outlined what I understood him to be working on, and how we could work together to resolve any disputes. My efforts to calm things down didn't work. The attorney's response email again tried to dredge up past issues and accusations.

I decided to not remind him that one of his first communications with prior counsel were to suggest that my client should be shot, not an idle threat in view of the attorney's past history of threatening a neighbor with a gun. That wouldn't help anyone at this point. Undeterred (yes, sometimes I think by sheer force of will I can keep people from being complete jerks) I responded back, again trying to lower tensions, but it never got any better. To this day, almost every communication is full of barbs and personal insults.

In fairness, I don't think that lawyers really understand why they become increasing more belligerent and hard to deal with over the years. No one teaches lawyers about the physiological effects of day-to-day lawyering, especially the dog-eat-dog world of trial lawyering. I had little idea of the effects on me until I had been practicing law for over 15 years. The physiological reactions I learned to recognize in FAST Defense simulated mugger attacks were the same as the contentious environment between lawyers. Increased heart rate, gross motor skills enhanced, fine motor skills reduced, tunnel vision, auditory exclusion, high brain function reverting to lower, primitive brain function-these all occurred in depositions and court. This is why I often could not remember things I said during heated exchanges in depositions, or sometimes even in arguments to the court. This is why I could not remember things that my client assured me they told me during deposition. It also explained why arguments so frequently broke out between lawyers during depositions. If you want to see a classic and oft-repeated example of such dynamics, check out this YouTube that went viral several years ago, Texas Style Deposition, https://www.youtube.com/watch?v=ZIxmrvbMeKc

> No one teaches lawyers about the physiological effects of day-to-day lawyering, especially the dog-eat-dog world of trial lawyering.

Being in an adrenaline-induced state of heightened awareness, sensitivity to threats, and reduced cognitive function, all feeds into bad behavior directed at other people.

To get a sense of this collateral damage, consider the example that played out with our cats. Our indoor cats were familiar and amicable with each other most of the time and had peacefully lived under the same roof for many years. However, there was a neighborhood cat who used to come trotting by the window, hissing and taunting the indoor cats. She was a real piece of work, this cat. I saw her do this at neighboring houses too. She would work the indoor cats into a frenzy and, with them unable to get through the glass to lash out at the real offender, the cats turned on each other, hissing, growling and fighting. In *Psycho Kitty? Understanding Your Cat's Crazy Behavior* the author discusses this phenomenon of redirected aggression and what mitigates and aggravates its effect.

> [I]f the cats are separated immediately after the incident, there's a good chance that all will be forgotten

by the next morning. Unfortunately, [if left together] they would remain agitated with one another. Long after the true trouble source has left the yard in search of other cats to terrorize, the two hapless companions remain at odds with each other.

We would like to think we are more advanced than cats, but think again. Much of the discourteous and downright mean behavior of lawyers interacting with other lawyers is fueled by the adrenaline rush of being woofed by another attorney, creating ripples and then tidal waves of dysfunction. If I as a lawyer am responding to opposing counsel as though they were out to do me bodily harm, then my discourse with them will be anything but civil and courteous. Furthermore, if the last attorney I talked to was rude to me, I am more likely to be rude to the next one. It becomes a cycle almost impossible to avoid, especially when you have to deal with the offending attorney over and over again for an extended period of time.

Here's but one example of an exchange between counsel that is contentious for no reason at all. This type of exchange happens all the time. The context was a court order that the parties provide periodic joint status reports to be filed in a case that was stayed during completion of another legal action. You would think that this would be a simple, non-contentious process. No. Any "joint" action by lawyers means it is fodder for endless arguments.

I sent a short draft document outlining the current status of a related case (no one had any dispute with that), and also contained a single sentence regarding the status of the case in which the report was being filed.

As indicated in the prior status report, Plaintiffs are willing to mediate this case as the Court suggested, but Defendants are not, so no mediation has been conducted.

Opposing counsel objected to that sentence. They didn't want the sentence at all, said it was inaccurate, and had nothing to do with the status of the case.

Having been told that my sentence was inaccurate, I asked for clarification.

> Could you clarify for me then about the mediation? It was my understanding that your clients were not amenable to mediation. Did I misunderstand?

Things immediately went downhill. I was accused of "avoiding the point," and engaging in "unnecessary and improper posturing." Opposing counsel wanted the sentence removed entirely.

I tried again.

> You did not answer my question about mediation— are your clients willing to engage in mediation or not? As to the joint report, since none of the Defendants want to include reference to the mediation status, I have separated that out into its own paragraph. Please confirm or provide any additional edits, and I'll get this report filed.

I had modified the sentence as follows.

> Plaintiffs also add (and Defendants refuse to join in this paragraph) that Plaintiffs continue to be willing to mediate this case as the Court suggested, but Defendants are not willing to mediate, so no mediation has been conducted.

The argument continued. This time they claimed the issue had been dealt with in a prior document, that my sentence was inappropriate, redundant, and they weren't going to rehash it.

I responded back.

> The Court's order reads as follows: "counsel shall file a joint report detailing the status of the case within 60 days and every quarter thereafter until the action has been reactivated." The inability to get the parties in front of a mediator as the Court suggested is part of the status of the case. I'm happy to distinguish that you are not agreeing with that paragraph—that is common in joint reports—but reference to the mediation is part of the "status of the case" and will be in the report.
>
> You have yet to answer my question - are you willing to engage in mediation?

We were now at Round #7 of a single sentence in a status report about a case in which nothing was happening. Opposing counsel snapped back, rudely telling me to do whatever I wanted. He indicated that he would prepare an additional document to attach to the joint report. As to mediation, he claimed he answered my question months ago (but didn't repeat what that answer was), and then claimed my clients surely weren't willing to mediate if we couldn't agree to the language of a joint report.

Perhaps it was just me, but this is not only bordering on the ridiculous, but was full-on absurd. I forged on. After all, the Court ordered us to file a joint report.

We are required to submit a joint report. You cannot unilaterally dictate its contents. I will not represent something as being your position if it is not, but that doesn't preclude the completion of a simple joint status report. I am sending you a third revision that makes more sense under the circumstances.

My third version of the single sentence now read as follows, with space beneath it for Defendants' position.

Plaintiffs' version
Plaintiffs continue to be willing to mediate this case as the Court suggested, but Defendants are not willing to mediate, so no mediation has been conducted. No settlement discussions of any kind have been had between the parties since the last hearing.
Defendants' version

Nope, that didn't end the argument either. You cannot "unilaterally dictate" things, both defendants want one thing, so you are the one being disagreeable, stop posturing. And they sent me another version of language.

Defendants' position, now version #4 of my original single sentence, not only objected to what I had written, but what the Court had originally ordered. They objected on the grounds of "improper summarization" and misrepresentation of a prior document, and, of course, complained about "posturing." They also argued that the court should change its order about requiring any of these joint reports at all.

I'm sure some of you reading this are thinking "why didn't they just pick up the phone and sort this out?" Yes, that sounds logical and all, but trust me, it wouldn't have made any difference whatsoever. God bless my client who had been copied on the entire exchange and sent me an encouraging note.

> I am amazed at how rude these guys are to you. They are demeaning and belittling in almost every transmission, attempting to make you seem as though you have no clue as to what you are doing.

The irony was that I was so accustomed to this type of exchange that it barely phased me. I have been awash in a sea of adrenaline for the past 20+ years. Adrenaline and its effects is the crushing elephant in the room of every courthouse across the country. Lawyers strung out on adrenaline, triggering each other over and over again, are crowding our courtrooms with lawsuits that never end, disputes that never get resolved, and leaving a wreckage of emotional trauma, because those entrusted to handle cases have a compulsive need to continue the fight-or-flight hormone rush within their own bodies. It is just as addictive as cocaine.

> Lawyers strung out on adrenaline have a compulsive need to continue the fight-or-flight hormone rush that is just as addictive as cocaine.

Solutions to this rampant problem are more likely to come from outside the legal profession than from within. The following is an observation from someone who has had a front row seat to several lawsuits.

> Here's my two cents for improving the legal system …—mandatory referees on all cases. The Referee makes

sure that attorneys are playing fair with each other and following the guidelines set forth by the judicial system. The Referee will see all materials exchanged during the case, not just the documents filed with the court. The Referee will also track deadlines for discovery, monitor depositions, etc. The Referee will score the attorneys and at the end of the case, the attorney will be rewarded or sanctioned. I think that would move the judicial process along quickly and make sure bad apples...are stopped and save the courts tons of money in wasted time, paperwork, ex parte hearings, etc.

— DeAnna McGough

THE EVILS OF FEE CUTTING

*"The evils of fee cutting ought to be apparent to all
members of the Bar...[T]the habitual charging of fees less
than those established [in minimum fee schedules]...
may be evidence of unethical conduct ... "*

-American Bar Association, *circa 1961*

One of the most frequent questions people have is "why do lawyers
cost so much?" One might jump to the conclusion that lawyers are
just greedy, but that isn't the reason, at least not the primary reason.
The history of *how* lawyers charge for their services and *how much* they
charge is a tortured path of twists and turns, none reflecting well on
the profession.

Once upon a time, there were statutory caps on legal fees. If
you can charge no more than $500 for a certain legal task, you are
motivated to complete it in a reasonable amount of time. Being
slow erodes the law firm's bottom line without negatively affecting
the client. By the 1940s, the nature of legal fees was changed from
being capped to having floors. State bars published minimum fees for

various legal tasks, and penalties were assessed to attorneys charging any less. Indeed, the ABA Model Code, in effect until 1969, declared it unethical to 'undervalue services.'"[13]

Let that sink in for a bit. The American Bar Association, boasting on its website of a membership of nearly 400,000 members and being "committed to supporting the legal profession" and "improving the administration of justice" made billing clients *more* rather than *less* an ethical mandate. The following is a quote from a 1961 ABA Opinion[14]

> The establishment of suggested or recommended minimum fee schedules by bar associations is a thoroughly laudable activity. The evils of fee cutting ought to be apparent to all members of the Bar. . . . When members of the Bar are induced to render legal services for inadequate compensation, as a consequence the quality of the service rendered may be lowered, the welfare of the profession injured and the administration of justice made less efficient. For example, no lawyer should be put in the position of bidding competitively for clients. It is proper for the profession to combat such evils by suggested or recommended minimum fee schedules and other practices which have a tendency to discourage the rendering of services for inadequate compensation. . . Direct or indirect advertising by whatever means that a lawyer habitually charges less than reasonable or minimum fees would, of course, be objectionable. . . .
>
> [T]the habitual charging of fees less than those established in suggested or recommended minimum fee schedules, or the charging of such fees without proper justification, may be evidence of unethical conduct . . .

In the early 1970s, however, the practice of minimum fee schedules was challenged as constituting price-fixing in violation of Section 1 of the Sherman Antitrust Act. In the case of *Goldfarb v. Virginia State Bar*[15], the United States Supreme Court ruled that the practice of law was not a "learned profession" exempt from anti-trust laws, but rather a "trade or commerce" whose minimum fee schedules were "a classic illustration of price fixing" and "unusually damaging" in terms of harming consumers.

Abolishing minimum fees, one would think, would make legal services more affordable. Unfortunately, the opposite occurred. Enter the concept of billable hours. Without caps or floors on legal fees, lawyers would assign "value" to their work by charging clients in terms of the "hours" it took to perform the work. Now, instead of inefficiency in work eroding the law firm's bottom line without negatively affecting the client, inefficiency was the key to law firms' financial success. Why charge a client only $300 for a task when you can be more meticulous (and slow) and charge them $3,000?

The shift to hourly billing meant that inefficiency would become the new key to wealth and success for lawyers. "How many lawyers to change a lightbulb?" "As many as you can pay for."

> The 1970s shift to hourly billing meant that inefficiency would become the new key to wealth and success for lawyers.

How much could a lawyer charge for the original apple pie agreement between John and Mary earlier in the book? Five bucks? The information necessary for drafting that two sentence agreement, perfectly satisfactory for John and Mary's purposes, could be derived from a high school business law class. When you've sunk tens of thousands of dollars (and often over 100 grand) on a legal education, you need to do a little more than simple transactions to make your legal education investment pay off. You need to do complicated things, things that take a lot of time, things for which you can bill a lot of money and which make you look indispensable to your clients.

Lawyering was no longer a "learned profession," but just another means of trade and commerce, and law firms competed with each other over how many billable hours, and profits per partner, they could make in a year. Associates were given minimum billable hour requirements that they must meet or exceed in order to keep their job, increasing over the years from an average of 1,300/yr to over 2,000/yr in many large firms. If you assume the associates worked 50 weeks of the year, 2,000 hours would be 40 hrs/week, a near impossibility to accomplish with spending any less than 50 hrs/week at the office to allow time for non-billable tasks, mandatory pro bono work, and other firm-related business.

HELPFUL HACK

Legal fees are negotiable between you and a lawyer. Don't agree to an amount or fee structure that you don't believe is fair or appropriate. Insist on as much specificity as possible on what legal matters will cost you so you can budget for them.

Bestselling author Sophie Kinsella, in her book *The Undomestic Goddess* tells the story of a young woman attorney in London working up the ranks at a prestigious law firm. Just as she is on the verge of partnership, she makes a catastrophic mistake with a filing deadline, runs away to the countryside, and gets a job as a domestic. Although the book is fiction, Kinsella's portrayal of Samantha, is dead-on accurate.

I'm not *addicted* to my watch. But obviously I rely on it. You would too, if your time was measured in six-minute segments. For every six minutes of my working life, I'm supposed to bill a client. ... When I first started at Carter Spink it freaked me out slightly ... I used to think: *What if I do nothing for six minutes? What am I supposed to write down then?* ... But if you're a lawyer at Carter Spink, you don't sit around. Not when every six minutes of your time is worth money. ... And the truth is, you get used to measuring your life in little chunks. And you get used to working. All the time.[16]

With the billable hour, lawyers become widget makers. The more widgets produced, the more money the firm makes. (Not the associates themselves, of course; they are on salary and exempt from overtime regulations.) Being competitive, driven, A-type personalities, however, it only made sense that someone would create a commercial market based around the fighting of these widget maker gladiator law firms for supremacy. Enter the *American Lawyer* magazine and its annual AmLaw 100 list ranking law firms.

⌐ HELPFUL HACK ¬

Don't be shy in asking the law firm you are considering hiring whether they have mandatory minimums of hourly billing for associates and, if so, how they are going to ensure that they work efficiently on your case. There are plenty of law firms who will take this question and these concerns seriously and work out fee arrangements that are cost-efficient to you or your business.

The *American Lawyer* magazine was founded just four years after the *Goldfarb* price-fixing lawsuit, and tracks and fosters competition between the largest law firms. It publishes annual AmLaw 100 and AmLaw 200 lists that rank US law firms by size (number of attorneys), profits per partner, and overall revenue. It should be little surprise that law firms suddenly grew into megafirms with thousands of lawyers, leveraging the labor of junior lawyers to continuously increase partner profits and overall firm revenue. Lawyers, naturally competitive as they are, eagerly jumped aboard this commercial enterprise to compete for the top spot, even in remarkably disingenuous and harmful ways. During the economic downturn around 2009, some of these practices started coming to light. For example, the dissolving 106-year-old law firm of WolfBlock, LLC was reported as using a line of credit at the beginning of the year to pay bonuses for the previous year. "'When they felt the real earnings were inadequate, they just borrowed to pay themselves what they thought they were worth,'" former chairman Robert Segal is quoted in the ABA Journal.[17]

What the AmLaw lists have done is create a hierarchy of law firm reputation based on two of lawyers' most prevalent vices— greed and competition. It has also fed the rapid descent in the quality of life for lawyers which, in turn, reduces the value of their services to clients. Lawyers spend so much time focusing on generating a product— billable hours—that they give little or no thought to whether clients need or want so many billable hours.

United States Supreme Justice William H. Rehnquist, in a 1986 address before the Indiana University School of Law, summed up the problem like this:

> It seems to me that a law firm that requires an associate
> to bill in excess of two thousand hours per year…is
> substantially more concerned with profit-maximization

than were firms when I practiced. Indeed, one might argue that such a firm is treating the associate very much as a manufacturer would treat a purchaser of one hundred tons of scrap metal: if you use anything less than the one hundred tons that you paid for, you simply are not running an efficient business.

Others have characterized work in "big law" as these megafirms are called, as "often grueling, hierarchical, mind-numbing, and, at times, downright dehumanizing."[18]

Billable hours have become a vicious task master hanging over lawyers' heads, encouraging them to abandon all life outside of the office in quest of squeezing the most hours, and thus the most money, out of the day. It discourages efficiency of work by definition (why finish a project in 8 hours if you can stretch it out to a 20-hour billable project?) and has no correlation to the "quality" of the work product. "Quality" is defined here as something of value or use to a client. Is the 20-hour brief a "higher quality" than the 8-hour brief? At best, the client will never know. At worst, it is blatant fee gouging.

This seems to be a self-evident fact, but despite all of the deriding of the system, even by many within the legal system, the billable hour model continues, practically unabated.

In the January 2009 issue of the California Bar Journal, the article "Will a bad economy force more changes in the profession?", Richard Gary of Gary Advisors, a former chair of Thelen, Reid and Priest, was quoted as thinking the billable hour isn't going to disappear.

We've been thinking about going to a different model for 20 years and it's never happened. Maybe young people will come up with a different mousetrap." However, [Mr. Gary] added, "I still think it's the best way to measure value because it is a mechanism of measuring the amount of work that a lawyer did for a client on a particular matter.

Hogwash! The amount of time spent on a project is not an accurate reflection of the end product's value and never has been. Lawyers have forgotten that basic truth because it is in their best interest to forget.

Early in my career I found myself as plaintiff's counsel in a small civil matter against a defendant who was a part-time lawyer who reveled in the opportunity to "practice" law. I vividly recall receiving a 25-page, single-spaced motion to dismiss the case. It was so painful to read I could only manage to digest a couple pages at any one sitting. My opposition brief was one page, double-spaced, setting forth the statute supporting my position. He probably spent at least 25 hours on his brief. I spent less than an hour on mine, including research, writing, typing, printing, signing, copying, and a casual walk down the block to personally file the papers at the courthouse. Despite his verbosity, I won the motion. Which brief was more "valuable"? The one that took the most time to prepare, or the one that successfully convinced the judge?

This type of billing also becomes excessive in light of the overall goal of the clients when they hired the lawyers. In another example of overkill, a federal judge in New York City found a $100,000-a-day fee application from law firm Dewey & LeBeouf for receivership work to be excessive. U.S. District Judge Denny Chin said that the fee request was "excessive in the context of a securities receivership where hundreds of victims of fraud have suffered substantial losses" and he questioned the firm's billing rates which were as high as $950/hr for some partners, $605/hr for some associates, and $285/hr for summer associates. Summer associates, by the way, are law students who have not even completed law school or passed the bar examination.

If you have any question about how stupid billable hours are, especially in litigation matters, call your kids in from the other room. You know, your kids who are squabbling over who has spent too much time in the bathroom or who borrowed the other's toy, clothes, or video game. Tell the kids you are instituting a new allowance structure. You will pay them to argue with each other. You'll pay them $5 a minute to call each other names, argue over everything they can think of, and not resolve any of their disputes. How much money do you think that will cost?

> If you have any question about how stupid billable hours are, tell your kids you are instituting a new allowance structure. You will pay them to argue with each other. How much money do you think that will cost you?

Law firm's addiction to AmLaw 100 prestige, however, mandates that these practices of ungodly billing rates and excessive hours continue on indefinitely. In 2014, O'Melveny & Myers, one of the AmLaw 100 firms, had a dip in gross revenue, profits per partner, revenue per lawyer, and attorney head count. Not to worry, however, *American Lawyer* reports that the firm is "refill[ing] a pipeline of high-end litigation work."[19] How eager would the lawyers in this law firm be to quickly resolve litigation for their clients? Resolution would end the flow of billable hours and would act as a drain on the "pipeline" of legal fees and undermining the law firm's AmLaw 100 status. For prospective clients of this firm (or any similarly structured firm), what is the selling point exactly?

Many law firms have many experienced and talented lawyers; those can be found anywhere. Does the firm's gross revenue infer better client service, though? Do profits per partner or revenue per lawyer bespeak quality of service to the client, or rather workaholic tendencies coupled with high hourly billing rates? And does the head count of lawyers in the firm help anything? Exactly how many lawyers are needed at any any given time anyway?

In the genius book "Rework" by 37signals founders Jason Fried and David Heinemeier Hansson, they sum up workaholism like this.

> Our culture celebrates the idea of the workaholic. . . It's considered a badge of honor to kill yourself over a project. No amount of work is too much work. Not only is this workaholism unnecessary, it's stupid. ... Workaholics wind up creating more problems than they solve. . . . They even create crises. . . . They enjoy feeling like heroes.[20]

Does that sound like lawyers? Absolutely! In fact, if you read the entirety of *Rework*, which I highly recommend, there are many more indictments of classic lawyer behaviors, like this one.

> If all you do is work, you're unlikely to have sound judgments. . . . You stop being able to decide what's worth the extra effort and what's not. And you wind up just plain tired. No one makes sharp decisions when tired. . . . Workaholics aren't heroes. ... The real hero is already home because she figured out a faster way to get things done.[21]

Not only do law firms mandate overwork in a general sense, they also stupidly overstaff litigation. Consider the almost universal practice in larger law firms of assigning many lawyers to a single lawsuit before even seeing if it will require much effort. I've been on the other side of these cases long enough to see the pattern. The first response to either a demand letter or a lawsuit complaint comes from a partner or high level associate, with the highest billable hourly rates in the firm. They are throwing their weight around, or trying to sweet talk the other attorney, especially trying to play up any perceived advantage of their years of experience or law firm size versus the other attorney's. The initial responses will be signed by the most senior attorney, but there will be two or three other associates also listed on the pleading documents.

This approach never has the intended effect. If an attorney has done his research and is ready to proceed with a lawsuit before sending a demand letter, having communications from a partner at any law firm is not going to be enough to convince them to pack their bags and go home. If it did, that attorney would not stay in business.

There's usually a month, maybe two, of this senior attorney (with the firm's highest billable hour rate) doing most of the work on the case. Then, invariably, when they have failed to get the plaintiff's attorney to go away, most of the work falls to the next junior attorney on the case, and after about six months, the cheapest and most inexperienced of the bunch. Why? Simple. At the beginning of the case, the law firm is catering to the client's emotional upset at being sued (and yes, even corporations get emotionally upset) and promise to "put their best man on it" to resolve the problem. The law firm also has received a substantial retainer that is burning a hole in the virtual pocket of their trust account. The sooner the money is "earned" the sooner they can transfer it into the law firm's operating account and add to the war chest of revenue that will help the firm maintain its AmLaw 100 status.

About a month or two into the case, however, the client has started getting the first few invoices and getting a little upset at the exorbitant amount of fees. After all, their initial emotional upset has been tempered somewhat over time and with the practical realities of the cost in money and business distraction that results from arguing the case. How can the law firm mollify their client? They can reduce the average monthly billings by using more of a younger associates' time while the partner goes onto the next case that he can siphon billable hours from before that case too gets passed on to lower level associates and lower billable hour rates.

The problem is further compounded, however, by these junior attorneys both having minimum billable hour requirements as a prerequisite to keeping their jobs, and having no incentive of any kind to streamline proceedings or actually work towards resolution of the case. The longer the case drags on, the easier it is to bill hours. Until the client draws a line in the sand and says "no more," the billing will go on perpetually.

Overstaffing has taken on epically foolish proportions during recent years during the economic decline of many segments of the economy that has impacted law firm work and revenue. Any ordinary business would put a freeze on hiring and start reducing hours or laying off people if the business needs did not warrant all of those people. Law firms, however, started paying new law graduates to *not work* for them. These are just a few reported examples.

> Any ordinary business would put a freeze on hiring if the business needs did not warrant all of those people. Law firms, however, started paying new law graduates to not work for them.

Stroock, Stroock & Levan offered to pay new law school graduates to whom they had extended job offers previously $50,000 to delay starting work from the fall of 2009 until January 2010, or $75,000 to find other employment.[22] Morrison & Foerster offered to pay $5,000 per month plus the cost of medical benefits to 2009 law grads who would defer their start date to January 2011.[23] And this came not long after summer associates paid around $3000/week, were complaining about "skimpy" lunch stipends of $55 and being plied with too much expensive food and alcohol by their law firm employers.[24]

Is it any wonder that legal costs to clients have been soaring out of control? Why does a law firm need to charge $400, $500, $600 an hour and more?

How can law firms afford to do this? One way is the ongoing development of a strict hierarchical structure for law firms, where invisible lawyers labor day after day in poor conditions, for insufficient pay, doing low intellect, high markup legal work, with no hope of ever rising to the level of a well-paid associate, much less partner, of the firm.

PEDIGREE OVER QUALITY— THE HIERARCHY OF LAWYERS

"It's not your blue blood, your pedigree or your college degree. It's what you do with your life that counts."

-Millard Fuller

Only 11% of all U.S. lawyers work for the largest 350 law firms in the country. This segment of the profession is referred to as "Big Law." Big Law gets the most press, the biggest clients, and highest hourly wages, and the highest profits per partner in the profession. BigLaw does not, however, hold a monopoly on skilled lawyers.

In BigLaw, pedigree still is the one and only real measure of whether a lawyer will get hired or be promoted. If you don't have the proper "pedigree," you can either join the remaining 89% of the legal profession in government, business, or small law firm practice, or you can get a job as an "invisible lawyer."

Law firm DLA was at the top of the AmLaw 100 list in 2013, with annual revenue of over $2.4 billion dollars. (No, that's not a typo—

billion, not <u>m</u>illion). DLA has 4,036 lawyers, so when you do the math, that's $604,683 per lawyer. Of the top 15 ranked law firms (on the criteria of profits per partner), partners received between $2.7M and just shy of $5M— per partner. How do they rack up such huge profits year after year? Okay, if you have over 4,000 workaholic lawyers churning out billable hours at obscene hourly rates, that helps. But that's not all that helps. These large law firms also maintain profit centers of low-paid, invisible lawyers.

This is part of the strict caste system of white shoe law firms and the untouchable, invisible workforce of highly educated, but insufficiently pedigreed, lawyers.

In the 1940s and 50s, New York law firms were like private clubs, reports Erwin Smigel in *The Wall Street Lawyers*, these law firms were looking for:

> Lawyers who were Nordic, have pleasing personalities and "clean-cut" appearances, are graduates of the "right schools," have the "right" social background and experience in the affairs of the world, and are endowed with tremendous stamina.

Sadly, very little seems to have changed since then.

Jeff Bleich, President of the California State Bar, wrote "Reflections on our Reflection" in the *California Bar Journal*, July 2008 issue, about how the makeup of the legal profession is a poor reflection on the diversity of our society as a whole. Looking at the portraits of prior presidents of the state bar, primarily white males, caused him to reflect on this.

> You can't look at that wall for long without wondering what the bar and what this profession lost decade after

decade. All of the talented men and women who were excluded from practicing law, or from the bar, or from leadership because of their race, their gender, their orientation, their disability. Decade after decade, our profession was deprived of their talents because of a culture of narrow-mindedness and bigotry.

One type of invisible lawyers are "contract lawyers," lawyers who have not gotten a job as an associate at a law firm, but instead are hired by legal employment agencies to work for law firms doing mind-numbing, grunt legal work, such as document review on massive litigation and due diligence on large transactions. This work is billed out to the client at hundreds of dollars an hour, but the contract attorneys get only a small portion of that money, have poor working conditions, no job security, and no hope of any advancement in the law firm no matter how hard they work. In fact, most don't even have any contact with the pedigreed associates and partners. These lawyers thought they were on the path to a successful legal career, but then ended up dumped into its sweatshops.

HELPFUL HACK

When negotiating an agreement with a law firm, make sure your contract specifies who will be handling your legal work, and make sure the fees are commensurate with that. If the law firm is sending your legal work to low-cost lawyers in India or basement dweller contract attorneys, but are billing you premium US partner and associate rates, you are paying more in legal bills than you should.

One such woman lawyer shared her story recently. She was working, via a temporary legal employment agency for $33/hr (trying to pay off a likely $100-$150K student loan) in a room off of a parking garage with no heat, no windows, no bathroom, no insurance, no paid holidays or vacations. She had no connection to the plush offices in the neighboring highrise building other than the case she was working on. It was a class action suit in which the highrise, white shoe lawyers were bound to reap large financial rewards, while the contract lawyers working in the dungeon below would be shuffled out the door without even a thank you to be herded into the next dungeon for another law firm. Contract lawyers aren't even entitled to overtime pay, said U.S. District Judge Richard Sullivan recently. Even if they are doing clerical work such as simple document scanning, the fact that they are lawyers exempts them from the protections of federal overtime provisions.[25] Fortunately, Judge Sullivan's decision was successfully appealed and the case sent back to the trial court for further proceedings.

Nobody goes to law school with the plan of working as a contract lawyer, but if you do not have independent sources of income (such as a trust fund), and you emerge from law school laden with debt, you'll take whatever job you can. Fresh out of law school and after passing the bar exam, new attorneys are eager to work as lawyers, to use all of the knowledge they gained in the prior three years, but also have the additional pressure of debt. The idealism of an attorney and practical reality do not always mesh. "At some point you have to pay your bills; you have to eat," said David Lola, the contract attorney that Judge Sullivan ruled against. "The common theme is desperation," said another contract lawyer.[26]

HELPFUL HACK

Instead of hiring the most expensive law firm you can find, take advantage of the current glut of highly educated lawyers who have not found jobs. Particularly if you already have more experienced lawyers working for you, supplement your personnel resources by direct hiring or retaining of these less experienced attorneys, avoiding the middleman markups of both a legal employment agency and law firm.

Before some contract attorneys or law firms start to angrily argue with me over the treatment of contract attorneys, let me clarify the difference between "contract lawyers" and "freelance lawyers." There are attorneys who want to have the flexibility that traditional associate jobs do not provide and thus do work on a non-employee basis directly with law firms. This type of lawyers I consider to be "freelance lawyers" to distinguish from the "contract lawyers" that work through an employment agency. Freelance attorneys tend to not have the same level of negative experiences or poor working conditions as often described for contract lawyers. Furthermore, U.S. Labor Department statistics confirm that working freelance tends to result in much greater job satisfaction than working for a temporary employment agency. Whether freelance or contract, however, the mere whiff of such activities dooms any alternative options for lawyers.

Working as a contract lawyer is the death knell to any chance of ever after being perceived as having the "pedigreed" status that would qualify an attorney for a BigLaw job. According to Gary Sedlick of the Lateral Attorney Report, "The truth is that some firms simply will not consider hiring a lawyer if her resume reflects one or more stints as a contract lawyer. Whether this is fair or not is beside the point. Some firms and lawyers have this bias."[27]

Think about that statement for a moment. Putting in an honest day's work creates a stigma that impairs a lawyer's ability to obtain another job. What does it say about a law firm that ranks "not working" as a superior job qualification to "working"?

> What does it say about a law firm that ranks "not working" as a superior job qualification to "working"?

What does it say about a law firm that ranks "not working" as a superior job qualification to "working"?

The racial and gender stereotypes that accompany this "pedigree" distinction must also be acknowledged. Women lawyers are more likely to seek out some type of alternative work arrangements because they are balancing home responsibilities along with their job. Furthermore, minority lawyers are disproportionately represented in contract lawyering jobs, or other types of legal work that are not on track for associate or eventual law firm partner status. The only known study of this type was done in 2007 by Joseph Miller, of JDWired.com.[28]

This insistence on "pedigree" over "quality" of lawyers continues even as the nature of the practice of law evolves. Ashby Jones at the Wall Street Journal Law Blog reported about a new firm using a different business model.[29] Axiom Global, Inc., he reported, charges corporate clients less by using more virtual practices, usually having their attorneys work at the client's offices, and use of a flexible staffing model. However, they still struggle with the perception of the quality of attorneys. "Axiom will have to continue to persuade the change-resistant legal world that its lawyers are good. 'I was skeptical at first,' says Xerox's Mr. Liu. 'I had to get over a fear that they weren't going to be as committed to the job or to the work as a permanent person.'"

Axiom's solution to this obstacle, however, smacks of the same snobbery that is the core problem—the desire for "pedigree" over "quality." According to the founder of Axiom, their biggest obstacle is "a lack of lawyers who fit its bill: pedigreed and law-firm-trained lawyers ready to jump off the traditional track."[30] Sherry Fowler (Sheherezade), in a candid blog post "Why Are Lawyers Such Snobs,"[31] laid the problem out with great clarity.

> [The legal profession] worships credentials. We assume people from big, fancy law firms are smarter, and we assume people from fancy expensive law schools are better. You're a big liar if you pretend its not true. . . .

A hierarchy of lawyers also extends beyond law schools and law firm reputation, and beyond the nature of their working arrangements. Types of legal practice have stereotypes that extend well beyond the confines of the legal world and extend to the general public.

One evening I was out with a group of friends and got engaged in a conversation which turned to what we each did for a living. I asked the guy I was chatting with to guess what I did. (I know, not a good idea, but I was curious). He gave it some thought and then said "You aren't a lawyer, are you? Because I hate lawyers."

I think he meant it as a joke. I grimaced. "Yeah, I'm a lawyer." His face turned a little red and he tried to save face. "Well, at least you aren't one of those trial lawyers."

The words were barely off his tongue when he realized his error. "Um, yes, I am a trial lawyer."

He should have known better, but he kept digging. He tried again, "But at least you don't do criminal law." "Well, yes, I do."

By this point you would think he'd know better than to continue, but he seemed determined to rehabilitate my image (and perhaps salvage any prayer of "scoring" with me) and kept going. "But you don't defend criminals, do you?" "Yes, I am a criminal defense attorney."

We both knew it was time to end this conversation, but he couldn't help himself from trying one more time to dig himself out of the massive crater he had dug for himself, "At least you aren't a public defender . . ." He looked up expectantly. "Actually, yes . . ." He turned and walked away.

Truth is that in some respects, criminal defense attorneys can be considered one of the purest callings in the legal profession, the "other thin blue line" working every day on the front line of preservation of our Constitutional system of justice, often working on behalf of people who cannot reward their efforts financially.

> Criminal defense attorneys have one of the purest callings in the legal profession. They are the "other thin blue line" working every day on the front line of preservation of our Constitutional system of justice.

IN DEFENSE OF PERSONAL INJURY LAWYERS

"Oh, I'm sorry. I forgot, I only exist when you need something."

- Unknown

I was watching a TV show the other day and the question to the contestants was "What kind of lawyer is the most hated?" The guesses were family law and personal injury. Personal injury won. In fairness, personal injury lawyers are probably not the worst; their job is simply misunderstood.

Here's the scenario with personal injury lawyers. John Doe has been injured in a car accident. First of all, he's upset that some other moron on the road caused an accident. Pretty much no driver will admit to being even partially to blame for any accident and John is no exception. From the beginning, John feels victimized and wants someone else to blame and expects that other person to own up to their irresponsibility by opening a checkbook and writing a big, fat check.

There's another dynamic at play here, too. An accident is a traumatic experience and, injured or not, he was surprised and put in fear of mortal danger. That takes awhile to process and deal with.

His injuries are painful and involve doctors who poke and prod and test him, adding more stress and indignity to the whole ordeal. Adding inconvenience to the injury, the doctor appointments interfere with even attempts at rest and recuperation.

John's injuries reduce his days at work. Maybe his absence irritates and inconveniences his boss and co-workers, or worse yet, he forces himself to work anyway while experiencing pain and discomfort. He comes home from work, exhausted and in pain, snaps at his wife and kids, who get cranky in response.

He tries to rest at night, but he can't get comfortable because of the injury, frustration at work, and fighting with his family. And the cycle repeats the next day, in a sleep-deprived state.

After a few days, reality starts getting a little blurred. Life was idyllic, indeed perfect, until some careless [he is sure to add some cuss words here] who didn't know how to drive ruined his entire life. He has been wronged! He's dealing with the emotional trauma of the accident, in pain, worried about when he'll get well, dealing with the financial and time pressures added by dealing with the accident, his work is suffering, his family is mad at him, he is sleep-deprived, and he may also be under the influence of painkillers.

Enter the personal injury lawyer. **Remember that the lawyer did nothing to contribute to the ills that have befallen John.**

John sees the lawyer because he needs some relief, he wants to be vindicated, feel better, get his life back in order, make the other driver pay, get medical bills paid, be sure any future medical bills are paid, and get his car fixed or replaced. He needs a savior, and the personal injury lawyer appears to be it. And miracle of miracles, the lawyer agrees to do all these things without demanding money up front.

Thus begins the descent down the rabbit hole. Although John signs a fee agreement saying that the lawyer will get a big chunk of any money recovered (30-40% is common) from the driver or his insurance company, in John's mind, the lawyer is a free miracle worker who will restored his shattered life.

A little dose of reality at this stage in the proceedings would go a long way to rehabilitate the reputation of personal injury lawyers. The work that they have agreed to do is neither free nor miraculous. Furthermore, the lawyer is running a business with overhead, bills, and expenses.

The personal injury lawyer cannot, under any circumstances get everything the client wants. The client wants the clock turned back to a fictitiously-sweetened version of life before the accident. Even if time travel were possible, John's life pre-accident was not near as idyllic as he now thinks. But even aside from that, there is no dollar amount that will truly make John feel "whole" after his life was put in disarray by an unexpected occurrence brought on by an irresponsible driver.

> The personal injury lawyer cannot, under any circumstances get everything the client wants.

Furthermore, the lawyer cannot simply snap his fingers and get a huge check in hand. Getting an insurance settlement for a car accident is a lengthy and time-consuming process involving collection of a myriad of records, compilation of a thick demand package for the insurance company, and discussions and arguments with insurance adjusters and medical providers, and others. All this paperwork is managed by office staff that get paid on an hourly or salary basis even though no money will come in from the case for months or more often years (and sometimes never). It is an increasingly prevalent practice among insurance companies to deny claims and a lawsuit has to be filed which involves drafting of court pleadings, conducting and submitting to paper discovery and depositions. It also requires out-of-pocket costs for experts and other litigation costs.

For the client, time passes with little interaction with the lawyer and usually no indication of what the law office is doing for them. There are no monthly invoices, no regular status reports on case progress. In John's mind, the lawyer isn't doing very much. Finally, the lawyer calls John and says he's negotiated a settlement for a dollar amount that John has never seen in one check or bank account before. He's either offended because it isn't a million dollars, or his brain becomes a little foggy over desire for those dollars (forgetting that there are bills to be paid with it). In either case, a deal is struck, papers are signed, a check is issued. John's mouth is watering in anticipation of the well-deserved vacation he is going to take once he has the money, but before he gets the check in his hand, the lawyers give him a sheet of paper with a breakdown of how that money is going to be taken away from him.

First, there is the lawyer's contingency fee. It looks huge. That which was so easy to sign away when it was a hypothetical amount of money, now feels like gouging and profiteering. He only saw the lawyer two or three times, the lawyer didn't almost die in a car accident, why should he get most of the money? And then there are expenses, medical bill liens, expert witness fees, deposition expenses. What had seemed like a large settlement dwindles to nothingness as John's eyes read down the page to the minuscule sum at the bottom listed as John's share.

John gets mad at the lawyer. And he tells his friends and family how greedy lawyers are and how they are worthless, crooked good-for-nothings. Lawyers jokes are shared and embellished, and personal injury lawyers fall into deeper disrepute.

But John's reality is only half of the story. What he doesn't realize (because the lawyer never explained it to him) is that from the lawyer's side of the table, he may have lost money on the deal and is currently nursing a beer at the local tavern pondering how he is going to meet payroll on Friday.

You see, contingency fee arrangements are bets. The lawyer is placing a bet that he can get a high enough settlement for your case (and the other cases the office takes) that the contingent fees cover the expenses, and turn some kind of a profit. When John came into the lawyer's office and signed the fee agreement, the lawyer was promising to spend time and out-of-pocket money without a guarantee of ever being paid for it. Cases are routinely lost for reasons that have nothing to do with a lawyer's expertise or diligence, and likewise, the dollar value of cases depends on many factors wholly outside of the lawyer's control. However, the lawyer's commitment is real, whereas John's is contingent.

What John forgets is that when he walked through the door of that law firm, he was in a deep hole. He had suffered financial and other harm caused by factors that were not caused by the lawyer. Whether it was maliciousness or carelessness of another person, or falls within the general category of "sh-- happens," damage had been done and John wants to be made whole and then some. The lawyer's job undertaken was to mitigate the depth of the hole, not fill in the hole and build a mansion on top of it. A personal injury settlement is meant to compensate for the damages—fill in some of the hole. If the lawyer managed to bring in a settlement sufficient to pay all the medical bills (and sometimes they can negotiate them down to low dollar amounts) and car repairs, and John gets a $100 bill to take the wife out to a nice dinner, that is still a win. It is John's expectation of a mansion that devalues the settlement. The paid medical bills are forgotten.

> The lawyer's job was to mitigate the depth of the hole, not fill in the hole and build a mansion on top of it.

So what are you to do when you find yourself injured in a car accident? Just take any money that the insurance company offers and forget it? Maybe not. Maybe a lawyer's involvement will help you get a better settlement offer, or help you get them to pay when the insurance company is offering nothing. Talk to your prospective lawyer. Offer to do some of the legwork in putting together the documentation necessary for the insurance company in exchange for a reduced percentage of the eventual payout in the case. Or understand that having the lawyer spend the time and money to assemble and pursue your interests is well worth a piece of the action.

REAL LAWYERS DON'T WORK
80 HOURS A WEEK

"For too many litigators, our life increasingly is a highly paid serfdom - a cage of relentless hours, ruthless opponents, constant deadlines, and merciless inefficiencies."

-Scott Turow, *"The Billable Hour Must Die"*

Have you ever noticed that the history of great lawyers never includes reference to the number of billable hours those lawyers accumulated? When you consider the greats—Abraham Lincoln, William Jennings Bryan, Clarence Darrow, Gerry Spence, for but a few—do you know what their billable hours were?

Of course not. Because great lawyers have great minds, can think well on their feet, and have excellent analytical and writing skills. Unfortunately, even the best of intellects fray with fatigue and lack of a balanced life style, a fact that the legal profession is slow to acknowledge.

An article titled "Billable hours 'intersect' with the profession's woes" in the January 2008 issue of the *California Bar Journal*, contains the now familiar story of a successful big firm lawyer who, after 16 years, had had enough. She wanted a life, she wanted a husband, she wanted children. Rather than being marginalized for working part-time for a big law firm, she opened her own consulting/mediation practice and works zero to 20 hours a week. She is hardly the only lawyer that has made that choice.

Although some law firms are claiming to make some efforts to create a more work-life balance friendly environment, they have a long way to go. Some years ago, at a work-life balance summit, no less, I heard a young associate from a large firm happily describe her 60% work week option as working "only 50 hours a week!"

Do the math on that option. If 50 hours a week is considered 60% effort (and worth 60% pay), her law firm is expecting over 83 hours of work a week as constituting 100%. That is more than two full-time jobs! Do you want your important legal work performed by somebody who has no life away from his desk covered with energy drinks and empty coffee cups? Is their time, each and every one of their hours, worth hundreds of dollars to you?

┌─ **HELPFUL HACK** ─

Before you sign a fee agreement, ask the law firm what their policies are on work-life balance. Do they expect their attorneys to be at the office six days a week? Can they assure you that the attorneys, more likely than not, have gotten a good night's rest the night before working on your important legal matters? Can they assure you that those attorneys will be rewarded, not penalized, for finding cost-saving legal solutions for you, rather than being expected to meet hourly billing quotas? If the law firm cannot give you acceptable answers, don't sign their fee agreement. Find another law firm.

Is it any wonder that lawyers suck??

For all the complaining about lawyers costing too much, what businesses need to realize is this one simple fact of our market economy—customers decide how much something is worth. Lawyers can be elitist and snobby all they want, but the sooner their clients refuse to buy into it, the sooner lawyers will change.

Remember *American Lawyer* magazine's AmLaw 100 list? AmLaw admits that their criteria for choosing "top" law firms (revenue per lawyer, profits per partner, and number of lawyers) is a "metric that has turned law firm managers into contortionists." They go on to credit increases in these metrics to (1) "surging demand for high-end legal services and unrelenting annual rate hikes," (2) a continuing slowdown in naming equity partners (the top echelon of law firms); and (3) increase in the number of non-equity associates. [32]

One may think that such attitudes cannot be changed, but I disagree. In January 2009 I wrote the following in a blog article—

> Clients who pay such excessive fees, however, especially large corporate clients, need to acknowledge their own role in encouraging outrageous billing by lawyers. Law firm prestige, and thus the law firms that tend to attract higher net-value clients, has for too long been measured on the same scale as Fortune 500 companies—by annual revenue. Not cost efficiency. Not creative thinking. Not being able to demonstrate insightful legal opinions. Not being successful in any other arena than extracting the most money out of their clients. . . .
>
> Corporate clients—the "surging demand for high-end legal services" is you, accepting the definition of "high-end" as being on the AmLaw 100 list. The "unrelenting

annual rate hikes" is the price you are paying for accepting this criteria. Rate hikes will keep increasing at these firms until you, the client, say "no." You are choosing "pedigree" and "prestige" over "quality" in legal services and have only yourself to blame for the outrageous legal bills on your desk.[33]

I argued that businesses can accept an ongoing competition between law firms over size and greed, a battle riled up by a magazine that benefits from the existence of the fight, or you can discard that and seek some other measure of value.

> If you choose "pedigree" and "prestige" over "quality" in legal services, you will only have yourself to blame for the outrageous legal bills on your desk.

Whether they read my blog or not, around that same time of economic downturn, many businesses did start changing their measuring stick for value. The Association of Corporate Counsel began an active quest to redefine the value of legal services with its "Value Challenge," pointing out the misalignment between what corporate clients want and need and traditional law firm business models. Corporate clients, ACC said, want

> [V]alue-driven, high-quality legal services that deliver solutions for a reasonable cost and develop lawyers as counselors (not just content-providers), advocates (not just process-doers) and professional partners. . . . [34]

Over the past several years, ACC has taken a very active approach in preparing resource materials and education for its members, inhouse counsel at major corporations, about various ways to implement the redefining of value and law firms are slowly, but surely, making adaptions.

When you select a lawyer for your own legal needs or for your business, keep in mind that you, and only you, define the value of your lawyer, and the fees you pay are negotiable. Shop around. Interview law firms and ask them how they approach handling of business disputes, how they staff their cases, how they measure a successful outcome for their clients. Ask them for price quotes for types of legal services you need presently, or anticipate needing. If they don't know how much things will cost, trust me, you won't like the invoices you receive.

One of the most valuable attributes of a good lawyer is the ability to be creative and resourceful in obtaining the end goals of their clients. If a law firm cannot demonstrate to you that they can meet these requirements, they aren't the right firm for you. If all they want to tell you is about their credentials and AmLaw ranking, you will know where their priorities will be in your relationship with them.

Why Lawyers Suck!

HOW I SETTLED A MILLION DOLLAR LAWSUIT WITH A $15 BOOK

"Creativity involves breaking out of established patterns in order to look at things in a different way"

- Edward de Bono

It would be impossible to overstate the impact that psychology and physiology have on the tone and duration of lawsuits. I have seen disputes drag on for months over a $200 difference in settlement positions. It makes absolutely no sense from an outside, objective perspective, but for the attorneys (and parties) engaged in the battle of a lawsuit, they can only see the narrow, tunnel vision, as frantic to win at all costs as if they were defending their very lives from an attacker. There are, however, some simple tools that can help you or your lawyer regain some perspective and plan a course towards resolution of disputes without all-out litigation.

I'll let you in on a little secret. I have a book on my bookshelf that contains the secrets to settling lawsuits. It's a book I bought on a whim on a trip to my local office supply store. It cost only $14.95, but it helped me settle a million dollar lawsuit.

> I have a book on my bookshelf that contains the secret to settling lawsuits . . . it cost $14.95.

It was a massive and complex lawsuit with both sides represented by teams of highly skilled, intense, competitive lawyers. The blitzkrieg of litigation warfare had been going on for many months with each round of interaction being more contentious than the last. Motions flew back and forth, discovery was disputed at every turn, tens of thousands of pages of documents were exchanged. The personal attacks between counsel became more and more vicious. It actually made me feel physically ill on many occasions. Don't get me wrong, I'm not saying that opposing counsel were mean bullies and I was an innocent victim. I was fully engaged in the nastiness, too.

One particular low point was a deposition where we all should have been nominated as poster children for bad lawyer behavior. There were arguments over the temperature in the room, when to go on and off the record, books that one attorney had sitting on the table, and one attorney's choice of clothing.

I'm sure you are laughing and shaking your head right now, but it's all true. At the end of the deposition, I swear it felt like an out-of-body experience, I found myself arguing with opposing counsel about what was to happen with one of the physical exhibits discussed during the deposition. Opposing counsel wanted to take it with him, I wanted it to remain with the court reporter, opposing counsel was instructing the videographer to take videos of the parts for us, and I told him that if pictures were adequate then he could have the pictures and we would keep the parts. It wasn't pretty.

What was the nastiness about? Simple. There was a lot of money at stake, and the clients on each side were willing to continue to fund the lawyers acting this way. Neither side wanted to show any weakness, any sign that the other side might interpret as willingness to not take this all the way to trial, appellate courts, or even the U.S. Supreme Court, if necessary.

Needless to say, there was simply no way we were making any headway towards settling the case; we could barely stand to be on the same phone line. That struck me as wrong because, fundamentally, I believe lawyers should be engaged in a professional, ongoing process of working towards case settlement. I didn't know how, though, not in this case. There had been too much water under the bridge by that point, too much vitriol. That's when I pulled the book off my shelf that had been sitting there for a least a year without being read—"Dealing with People You Can't Stand" by Dr. Rick Brinkman & Dr. Rick Kirschner.

In their book, Brinkman and Kirschner discuss 10 categories of difficult people on a continuum from passive to aggressive behavior, and from being task-focused to being people-focused. Four intentions, they explain, drive people's behavior.

- Get the task done
- Get the task right
- Get along with people
- Get appreciation from people

These are not personality types, such as in Myers-Briggs personality tests. Instead, they focus on behavior, noting that there is a normal zone of behavior for each person, and then exaggerated behavior, often exhibited when the person is under stress, that becomes their bad behavior (at least in the eyes of the people interacting with them). They point out that these intentions often change over time and in different environments, but people tend to have their preferred modes of dealing with things, thus resulting in the 10 categories. People with the intent to "get it done" can be controlling and aggressive. The intent to "get it right" leads to passive perfectionism. The intent to "get along" is people-focused and sometimes comes at the expense of the task being done right. The intent to "get appreciated" can be aggressive and attention seeking.

Looking at their description of these interactive intents, I recognized myself as being a "Tank" as a litigator. A "Tank" is task focused and aggressive, they want to get things done, and they interact with others in their way with the sheer focus and intensity of a tank on a battlefield, not requiring perfection, not much worried about people who might get run over in the process.

In explaining how people can work around this nature in me, the book offered some sound advice. "Don't be tempted to counterattack" because I would just escalate. So true. Lawyers who tried to attack back with naked threats, motions or discovery disputes just found themselves up against a more motivated me on the other side. "Don't try to defend, explain, or justify your position." True, I viewed that more as a sign of weakness than anything else.

I figured it was worthwhile to see if I could identify the mode that opposing counsel was working in and try to use the book's advice to turn the tide of intractable warfare in this lawsuit and at least start a conversation about settlement. I did some online investigation about my opposing counsel, found out more about his career history, his family background, activities, and other details that might paint a likely background and context to the behavior that was so offensive to me. It didn't take too long to figure out what his motivations likely were.

First of all, he was certainly aggressive in his interactions; no passivity from him. He was always on the attack. But was he task focused or people focused? Based on his family and career history (yes, I did lots of research) I saw a picture of someone needing to be noticed and acknowledged for his work and skill. For a moment I actually felt some compassion for him. It had to be very hard growing up in a family of lawyers, probably feeling he had to compete for attention and recognition among the rest. Perhaps he just needed some acknowledgment of his efforts from me (perish the thought) to turn around this situation.

I carefully read the Action Plan laid out in the book for dealing with the type that I had identified—"The Think-They-Know-It-All." Step 1 was to "give them a little attention." The very thought galled me. "He's a complete jerk, why should I give him some attention? I just want him to go away!!" But what could it hurt? Nothing else I was doing was working, in fact everything I had tried had been counterproductive. Maybe I could just take a chance and try what the book recommended. If it didn't work, it didn't work, and nothing would have been lost.

Following the book's recommendations was a little more challenging than I had bargained for, though. I argued them all in my head.

"Backtrack their comments with enthusiasm." No, absolutely not! I'm not going to highlight and affirm the ridiculous stuff he says! That will just encourage him.

"Acknowledge positive intent rather than wasting your time with their content." Seriously? I considered abandoning the book entirely. I did not discern any positive intent on his side. Wouldn't I be lying if I "acknowledged" something that I didn't consider to be there at all?

"Clarify for specifics." Okay, now there was something I could do without feeling I was dignifying anything he said or betraying my client. Just ask for specifics (and then hang him with them, I thought). That can't do any harm.

"Tell it like it is." That was not a problem; I could direct his attention to the reality of the situation.

"Give them a break. . . . resist the temptation to embarrass them." I was in no mood to give opposing counsel "a break" on anything, but I did have to acknowledge the wisdom here. If you get what you want (in my case, open the door to starting settlement discussions), don't gloat.

I sat down at my computer to write the letter to opposing counsel. I think that acknowledging positive intent in this jacka--was the hardest thing I have ever done in my career. Somehow realizing that he needed acknowledgement made me much more resistant to giving it. The wounds from his barbed comments and behavior were too fresh, too painful. But I had committed to myself to complete my test of the book's theory. I wrote a letter that opened with a statement of acknowledgment of positive intent and went along from there. Meaningful settlement negotiations ensued not long thereafter and finally, after a number of months of back and forth, a final deal was struck.

What is so interesting to me about this is the fact that this agonizing change in my approach at the time, was barely perceptible to the objective eye. As I was compiling materials for this book, I was long past the daily adrenal stress of that lawsuit and because of that I had a hard time even identifying from my files the letter that changed the course of my interaction with opposing counsel. The shift that had seemed so dramatic to me at the time was actually very subtle in retrospect. The turning point phrase looks benign now, a mere sentence fragment. "I appreciate your efforts."

Sometimes an agonizing change in approach while you are in the midst of heated litigation is barely perceptible to an objective eye.

Dealing With People You Can't Stand remains on my bookshelf to this day. It is well worn with post-it notes marking key sections and as I flip through the pages I am reminded of other instances where its advice turned the tide in contentious litigation. Another example was a mid-sized case that had been dragging on forever with no one budging on settlement for over a year. I finally suggested that opposing counsel and we should start having anniversary parties to celebrate the length of our "relationship" with each other over this dispute. It got a laugh, reduced tensions, and not long afterward, settlement negotiations brought the matter to a close.

At the end of the day, lawyers are just people. If you get them riled up, they will act irrationally and spend their client's money fighting battles not worth fighting. With even a small amount of people smarts, however, disputes can be de-escalated and resolved. Creativity, it turns out, is much more valuable to clients than thousands of hours of legal analysis and wrangling.

> At the end of the day, lawyers are just people. If you get them riled up, they will act irrationally and spend their client's money fighting battles not worth fighting.

SEEKING NEEDLES IN HAYSTACKS

"The true sign of intelligence is not knowledge but imagination."

-Albert Einstein

Finding a good lawyer who provides you with value for your money may seem like the proverbial quest for a needle in the haystack. Hopefully the preceding chapters and hacks have given you some tools to make the work easier, and this chapter will provide some additional considerations.

Redefining the "value" of lawyers is admittedly not easy. Different lawyers get paid in different ways for different types of work, and that is how it should be. Aligning the interests of reducing conflicts, finding simple solutions to problems, and yet having enough financial incentives for lawyers to go through the time and expense of law school is not easily done. Let me give you an example.

Early in my legal practice I specialized[35] in criminal defense, including DUIs. I handled enough DUI cases in the same county court to know, with almost mathematical certainty, precisely what would happen to a first-time offender charged with DUI. They would be sent for an alcohol evaluation, then would receive a fine and probation, and if the alcohol evaluation warranted it, getting some treatment would be part of the probation conditions.

I also knew the defenses that could be used to fight a DUI charge—an improper traffic stop, improperly performed sobriety tests, improperly performed breathalyzer test—and knew the physiology of alcohol in the body, how alcohol levels in the blood actually increase in the hour after ingesting the last drink, how men metabolize alcohol differently than women do, yada, yada, yada.

I knew all of the usual excuses and stories given to police officers by people stopped for suspected drinking and driving. My favorite was the "but I just had one beer" line, as though the officers didn't know that in this college town there were many bars that featured enormous beer glasses, such that "one beer" was the equivalent of a six-pack.

One day I received a phone call from yet another DUI defendant seeking representation. I asked all the relevant questions, about the stop, alcohol ingested (how much and when), the results of the sobriety tests and breathalyzer, and existence of any prior criminal record. After a half hour conversation it became clear to me that this potential client had no plausible defense, but with no prior record, would not be sent to jail. I explained my evaluation and recommended that they plead "no contest" and told them what the sentence would be. They said "thanks" and I hung up the phone. I just spent half an hour of my hard-earned expertise, the DUI defendant received a huge benefit, and I received no financial compensation at all. I realized this was no way to run a business, even though free consultations were the norm for this type of case and in this jurisdiction.

How then should a lawyer run a business? What is a fair and reasonable value for a lawyer's services? The silly notion that the best measure of the value of a lawyer's services is the amount of time spent multiplied by an hourly rate should have already been discarded after reading prior chapters.

Look for law firms that have alternative billing rates to straight billable hours with no commitment to you on how the time will be limited. For standard, routine legal work (for example, drafting a will or basic business contract), look for flat fees. If the law firm doesn't yet know approximately how much time this should take and have a flat fee reflective of that, it is either a very new firm, or not very enlightened. If it's a new firm, no worries. Ask for a cap on hours for the work that you can live with. If they want your business, now and in the future, they will likely agree and just eat any excess hours above their estimate.

Although the amount of time needed for litigation matters is harder to predict, press the law firm to break down their fee structure to put in as much predictability as possible. This can be done by outlining known activities in the case. Again, if a litigation firm cannot provide you with a firm price for activities that happen in every lawsuit, such as drafting a complaint, conducting an initial round of discovery requests, or similar activities, expect outrageous bills. Especially in litigation matters, be sure to ask whether law firm associates have billable hour requirements. If they are constantly needing to bill hours, don't be naïve enough to think that your case won't be the subject of "killing time billing" when the associate needs to bulk up his or her hourly billings for the month, even if the work isn't particularly helpful to you, the client.

When seeking legal representation, remember that prestige via law firm rankings, as discussed earlier, has no reflection on quality of lawyers. What then should take its place? There are no easy answers. There is a woeful lack of core information available to prospective clients of law firms that will meaningfully inform them of their choices in counsel. Unlike other industries who have carefully honed the process of advertising their benefits to customers, lawyers know little about marketing.

> Unlike other industries who have carefully honed the process of advertising their benefits to customers, lawyers know little about marketing.

Until the 1972 Supreme Court case of *Bates v. State Bar of Arizona*[36], lawyers were prohibited from advertising at all and many restrictions on advertising still remain. That's right, it took until 1972 for lawyers to be freed from a ban on advertising because such bans violated free speech, and also because Arizona's bar ban at issue "inhibit[ed] the free flow of information and ke[pt] the public in ignorance."

State bars are still allowed to regulate lawyer advertising. Some have such burdensome rules and requirements (including prohibitions on testimonials from prior clients), that often lawyers just throw up their hands in despair and just hope for clients to show up at their door. Therefore, don't expect lawyer advertising to follow similar lines as routine business marketing practices; the lack of a polished advertising for a law firm really means nothing in terms of quality of the attorneys. Look deeper than that.

Satisfied prior clients are excellent sources of new business referrals. However, for lawyers, such recommendations are supposed to be hidden behind closed doors. Ask your friends and colleagues for lawyers with whom they have had a positive experience, and go one step further to inquire why. A lawyer who is excellent for a divorce case is unlikely to be a good choice for incorporating a business, for example. Find out how much they charged in legal fees vs. perceived benefit. Maybe someone charged $500/hour, but was so efficient they did a better job than another lawyer who only bills $200/hr. Here in San Diego, California, there is a lawyer, Mr. Traffic Ticket, who charges $99 for handling most traffic ticket matters. Any other attorney who would even be willing to handle a traffic ticket matter would charge at least $500. However, Mr. Ticket's office handles only traffic matters and does it with incredible efficiency and skill. Better price, better quality services— I'll pick Mr. Ticket anytime.

Do not fall into the trap of judging a lawyer's abilities based on the source of their law degrees. Law schools, like law firms, are ranked every year, in the schools' case, by the U.S. News and World Report.[37] The rankings are then divided into "Tier One" and several other tiers that nobody is going to bother to advertise. Out of curiosity, I did a little research regarding the tiering of law schools; it was disturbing. This ranking system has been widely criticized and is not endorsed by the American Bar Association or the Law School Admission Council. The Association of American Law Schools, via its executive director Carl Monk, is cited as saying that "these rankings are a misleading and deceptive, profit-generating commercial enterprise that compromises U.S. News and World Report's journalistic integrity." I absolutely agree. It is the same type of enterprise as the American Lawyer's AmLaw 100 lists.

Notwithstanding this, the ranking game continues to be played, though sometimes with new twists and turns. It seems that U.S. News wants to include part-time students in its ranking process, which could prompt some law schools to drop such programs in order to keep up their rankings because part-time students don't fit into the same profile as full-time students. According to Daniel D. Polsby, dean of George Mason University School of Law in Arlington, Virginia,

> At every law school I know with a part-time program
> you are talking about [students who are] older, racial
> or ethnic minorities, people with jobs and families,
> people with interesting life experience that kids who
> are just past adolescence can't be expected to have," he
> said. 'Their college records are many years in their past
> [part of US News ranking criteria] and a less impressive
> measure of the law student he or she will be. Shutting
> them out will damage the profession.' [38]

We have now come full circle, haven't we? If you don't have a proper "pedigree" you can't get into the high-ranked school, if you can't get into the high-ranked school, you can't get the mega-bucks BigLaw job, and because you can't get the mega-bucks BigLaw job, your law school ranking falls. Non-traditional lawyers, those with diversified work experience outside of the legal realm, racial and ethnic minorities and women, then become increasingly underrepresented in the ranks of lawyers.

Public distinctions in the legal profession suffer from the same stereotypes and exclusive practices as the ranking systems. Relying on distinctions for achievement in the legal profession, you know, those pretty certificates on lawyers' walls, may mean nothing at all in terms of quality. Such "distinctions" are often simply for sale to the highest bidders.

> Distinctions for achievement in the legal profession
> often is for sale to the highest bidders.

For example, how does a women lawyer achieve distinction as a leader in her profession? You might be surprised at the answer that arrived in my mailbox one afternoon. "In recognition of Women's

History Month, women attorneys who have achieved leadership status will be profiled with bios," etc. in a future issue of the LA/Los Angeles Times Magazine. This opportunity was described in a colorful brochure as "the perfect way to salute those high-achieving women who are excelling in their professional roles."

"Wow!" I thought. "What a great idea! It is about time women lawyers who are making a positive impact on the legal profession get some recognition. What is the criteria for selection of these attorneys?" My jaw dropped as I read further. It appears that the one and only criteria for selection of these "high-achieving women" was payment of between $8,000-$55,000 (early bird discounts were, of course, available). Lacking $8,000 to buy distinction in the legal profession, I guess I'll have to settle for the heartfelt appreciation clients have expressed to me over the years.

Online resources for obtaining lawyer referrals are popping up these days that may or may not be helpful. As with the paid-for distinctions in legal magazines, inform yourself about the criteria for being listed. Do the lawyers pay to be listed, pay more for more prominent listings, or do they contribute comments or posts to "earn" a more prominent ranking? More importantly, what does the information listed really give you in terms of evaluation of competence, competitive pricing, or work efficiency and effectiveness? Use these online directories with care, ensuring that you have received more information about the lawyer from different sources before you decide which lawyer is best for your present legal needs.

JD Supra.com is an online directory of lawyers with samples of their work for prospective clients to view. Aviva Cuyler, a San Francisco-based attorney who founded JD Supra, said she was hoping to create "a central hub for information about the law and the people behind it."[39] It is at least one place where potential clients and other lawyers can see and evaluate samples of an attorney's work. I was among the first adopters of JDSupra and continue to maintain a profile and work samples on the site. Does this create a level playing field for lawyers from all sizes of law firms to show their skills to potential clients? Perhaps. JD Supra permits potential clients to see examples of actual work product, legal writing skills, transcripts of court hearings, court orders successfully obtained, and deposition transcripts. However, there are downsides there too. JD Supra has to turn a profit, and over the years large law firms having the funds to pay more money for subscriptions have, in my opinion, somewhat monopolized the attention of would-be clients and the media with profiles and work samples from their thousands of attorneys and, unfortunately, the little attorney without a marketing budget will have his or her skills buried in the sheer volume of BigLaw marketing.

I would like to see an annual Lawyer Olympics event where lawyers come together and demonstrate their skills in the areas of legal research, writing, oral advocacy, dispute resolution, and client counseling skills. Instead of relying on the law school grade or AmLaw law firm rankings, let potential clients see lawyers in action in a competition for skill and effectiveness.

Before you delve into the internet jungle of attorney directories and brokers, there are a few things to consider. First, find out who owns and runs the website and how they make money. The commercial interest of the entity compiling the information is an important factor in determining reliability and usefulness of the information. It illustrates their motivation to be accurate, current, and fair.

State bar attorney directories list lawyers who are legally authorized to practice in their state. Lawyers are often legally required to keep their information up-to-date, can be disciplined for misconduct, and if not properly licensed can face criminal penalties for unauthorized practice of law. I would consider these directories to be the most accurate sources of basic confirmation of authority to practice, but they don't contain much other information. References to "specialty" or "certified specialist" in these directories refer to special testing in particular areas of the law. These extra designations do not exist for every area of practice, and due to the extra cost, many lawyers don't bother with getting such a designation even if they are experts in certain areas.

Martindale-Hubbell, now www.martindale.com, is one of the oldest lawyer directories in existence. They once published thick books listing lawyer and law firm qualifications and sample clients. Now like everything else, their directory is online. This directory may provide a little more information than a bar association directory, but because lawyers have no requirement to keep information updated. While writing this book, I checked my profile. It contained my name and city where I was located, but a long outdated address. It listed an "overall peer rating" for me of "2.9 out of 5" which apparently "Meets Very High Criteria of General Ethical Standards." Well, I do try. As to experience & credentials, it accurately listed the states in which I am licensed to practice (though it did not distinguish between California where I am active and Nebraska where I am inactive). It offered a link to contact me. I was naturally interested in knowing how they intended to contact me when they didn't even have my address correct—something publicly available on the California State Bar website—so I sent myself a test message. Amazingly I promptly received an email, though it was marked as potential phishing.

An interesting note as to Martindale-Hubbell—they used to have a three-tier rating system for attorneys. Lawyers were either unrated (everyone started out unrated), and then progressively could get a CV-rating, then BV-rating, and eventually some got an AV-rating. I had been practicing law for around 5 years when I received notification from Martindale-Hubbell that I had received a CV-rating. Although I had not a clue why I had that rating, the fact that other attorneys I knew with more experience having no rating at all made me think it was something pretty exciting. However, I declined the corresponding offer to buy the lawyer directory that had my name in it, or the nifty plaque for my wall. Years passed. Somewhere around 10 years into my practice, I received another notification from Martindale-Hubbell advising me that I had achieved a BV-rating. Cool! Still didn't know why, still declined buying the book or plaque for my wall. A couple of years ago I received another notice, this time via email (of course), again offering me a plaque to honor my recognition as an "AV Preeminent Attorney." Way cool, at least I'm sure that's what they thought would make me want to buy a plaque.

Apparently my unwillingness to buy a book or plaque, no matter how highly I was ranked, was the final straw for my Martindale rankings. Further research revealed links to preview the certificates I could order for past recognitions. I appreciate the offers, but I'm still not buying their plaque.

Martindale contains an extensive discussion of their peer review rankings on their website, explaining a numerical system (1 to 5), with 1.0-2.9 being "Rated" (apparently as good as I get), 3.0-4.4 is BV Distinguished®, and 4.5-5.0 being AV Preeminent®. Ratings are determined through anonymous client reviews (they verify that these are from live persons, but cannot verify whether they are actual clients) and peer review (anonymous lawyers and judges). An unexplained review of unspecified information by an anonymous person is not something I would blindly rely on in selecting a lawyer.

Before I move on to discuss some other online directories, I make this note of caution. Some directories are owned by each other, and thus just regurgitate the same information (or disinformation, as the case may be). Avvo.com is a partner of Martindale-Hubbell according to their site. Lawyers.com is also part of Martindale-Hubbell. Because of this, don't use one to buttress the credibility of the other.

Some lawyer directory websites, such as Nolo.com, are what I like to call "pay-to-play." Attorneys pay to have their profile listed. The only thing you can definitively determine from such sites are that the lawyers listed are willing to pay to have a profile listed on that site. This could mean they are savvy about internet marketing or desperate for clientele, or it could mean they can't get enough word-of-mouth references. Treat these profiles as a lead, but don't hire one without doing some additional, independent research.

Some sites have a mixed model: every lawyer gets a simple profile, but also has the option to pay or contribute content to the site to get enhanced visibility. This is the Avvo.com model. Avvo has caused a great deal of commotion in legal circles for various reasons. For one, lawyers have no option of whether or not to be listed on the site. Avvo acquired bar information about every lawyer in the country and posted it, then added rankings and tried to get lawyers to opt-in and add additional information to increase their rankings. That did not sit well with a lot of lawyers, including me.

In 2010, I got into a public, online argument with Josh King, General Counsel & VP, Business Development, of Avvo. Avvo had posted inaccurate information about my law practice on my profile on their website and refused to change it unless I "claimed" my profile, an irrevocable action that would then entitle them to evaluate my credentials using their "secret sauce" algorithm to assign a number to me. I didn't want a "secret sauce" algorithm applied to my many years of legal practice. They didn't want to change the inaccurate information.

I sent a formal written demand to remove erroneous profile information. No response. Then in an online discussion thread following a blog article about Avvo, I publicly requested Josh King (who was engaged in the discussion) to remove the erroneous information from my profile. Still no change. Finally, I posted on Twitter that Avvo refused to remove erroneous information. That got a response. In less than an hour my profile had been edited to remove the erroneous information.

This was my problem with Avvo—its ranking system. Avvo got its database by acquiring official attorney registration files from state bar associations. They then published profiles and ask the attorneys to "claim their profile" and add more information. "Claiming" is an irrevocable act—I read the fine print. The method by which they assign numerical rankings from that info? It's a secret. They call it their "secret sauce."[40] A lawyer's ranking is directly connected to the amount of information the lawyer adds to Avvo's profile, thus having the effect of increasing rankings for lawyers who give stuff (information) to Avvo and depressing the rankings for lawyers who choose not to give stuff (information) to Avvo. It is a marketing platform, not a neutral database of information.

To date I have refused to "claim" my profile or accept any of Avvo's marketing offers. As I write this book, Avvo has designated my ranking as 6.9/10. They have also listed my practice areas as litigation, business, licensing, contracts/agreements, and intellectual property. I'm sure I could increase my ranking number if I play Avvo's game and "claim" my profile and add information about honors given, books written, and speeches made, but I don't want to, and I'm not the only lawyer who feels that way. If I don't know what 6.9 means, how do you as a prospective client? Furthermore, my practice areas are not as stated. I will say, however, that I appreciate that posted along with my mysterious "number" and inaccurate practice description are two wonderful client reviews— "Best Legal Service In California" and "Champion for the Client" and, my favorite review of all from an opposing counsel— "I endorse this lawyer. Had a trial against her and she was excellent." I also appreciate that the fine print terms and conditions for Avvo now seem to allow an attorney to opt to not have the numeric score published. That is progress.

As old fashioned as it sounds, often the best way to find a great lawyer is by word-of-mouth referrals from people you trust, but I have a little twist on the process for you. Don't expect that your friends and family will necessarily know a lawyer with the expertise you need, nor the interpersonal skills you want. However, their lawyer referral may know a lawyer who knows one in the area of expertise that you need. Invite them to direct you to someone who specializing in the type of legal need you have. Most lawyers are very willing to recommend trusted colleagues or even opposing counsel from another case, knowing that they will get appropriate referrals back. You can also use this process to find the best price point for lawyer fees. If you cannot afford to hire a large law firm at $500 or $600/hour, don't be shy in asking them if they can recommend a law firm that charges less. Frequently large law firm lawyers will refer clients who cannot pay their fees to younger, less experienced lawyers who can do just as good a job, but for a lower fee. Finally, interview several lawyers before you make a final decision. Even if they charge something for a consultation, it is worth the money to get a better feeling of which lawyer is going to be the best choice for you.

SHAKESPEARE WAS WRONG

"Kill all the lawyers."

—William Shakespeare

"Not so fast."

—Melody A. Kramer

I was a college freshman in Lincoln, Nebraska in 1985 when 68-year-old Helen Wilson was brutally raped and murdered inside her apartment in the nearby town of Beatrice. It was one of those heinous crimes that make you lose faith in humanity and demand that justice be done. Little did I know at the time how my life would intersect with that event.

Four years later, six people were convicted of committing the crime together, three men and three women. By the media they were dubbed the "Beatrice Six" and to some also dubbed the "Sara Lee Killers" referring to the evidence that the perpetrators made coffee and had pastries in the kitchen after the crime.

Five of the accused confessed after intense interrogation by police. Only one, Joseph White, went to trial. The jury convicted him and, although the case was death-penalty-eligible case, he was instead sentenced to life imprisonment. There was a certain sense of justice having been done for Mrs. Wilson and I gave no further thought to the case.

More than 10 years after the murder, I had graduated law school and was practicing criminal law in Lincoln when I got a letter of inquiry for representation on a post-conviction matter from an inmate. The inmate? Joseph White. I was intrigued.

I went over to the Nebraska Penitentiary and met him. As I walked into the visitor's room and saw him for the first time I knew, without a shadow of a doubt, that this man had not killed another human being. I have met other people who have and, trust me, you can see it in their faces. Joseph White was not a rapist or a murderer. Proving that, however, would be no small feat. Once someone has been convicted of a crime, it is very hard to overturn that decision.

For the next number of months I worked through the process of accessing and reviewing all of the information about his case, including the trial transcript. I was appalled. One of the primary witnesses at trial was one of the five suspects who had entered into a plea bargain. She described her state at the time of her apprehension and days of interrogation by law enforcement. She was a hard-core drug addict with hallucinations and was shown photo after photo of the gruesome crime scene. She testified that at a certain point she didn't know the difference between hallucinations and reality. This was a key piece of testimony and her description of her own mental faculties went to the very heart of the rules that govern trials—witnesses must be competent to give testimony. They must have the ability to comprehend and recall facts. She admittedly could not. She never should have been allowed to testify at all, but she had.

Another thing attracted my attention—there was no physical evidence that Joseph White had ever been at the scene of the crime. No fingerprints, no blood, no DNA. DNA testing was not commonly done at the time the crime occurred, but with no fingerprints and no blood (when samples of both were found at the scene) it troubled me that Joseph White was even charged with the crime.

I did my best to work through the materials and put together a successful post-conviction motion to overturn his conviction, but I was young and inexperienced and was not able to get the expertise needed to assist in getting the job done. I even reached out to Barry Scheck, of OJ Simpson's trial fame, but was not accepted for handling by the Innocence Project that he ran. My work was left incomplete when I relocated from Nebraska to California. One of my great regrets has been that I had been unable to take the necessary steps to overturn his conviction.

I went on to a new life with a new law practice in San Diego doing patent infringement litigation, a far cry from the days of being a criminal defense attorney. Then, one day in 2011, I received an email from a lawyer in Nebraska, a lawyer for Joseph White. "I don't know if you are aware, but Joe and the other 5 who were convicted, were exonerated regarding the death of Helen Wilson."

I sat at my desk stunned, relieved, grateful for the new lawyers who had done what I could not do, find a way to exonerate Joseph White. It pains me to this day, though, that it took so long. In 2008, after a battle all the way up to the Nebraska Supreme Court to access evidence for DNA testing, DNA testing was done that excluded all six of the Beatrice Six as being involved in the crime, and also identified the real perpetrator of crime, a man who had died a few years previous while incarcerated for another crime.

Joseph White had been imprisoned for 19 ½ years for a crime he did not commit. The Beatrice Six were the first people exonerated by DNA evidence in Nebraska history, and the largest number of defendants in one case exonerated by DNA testing in the United States. The six defendants were wrongly imprisoned for a total of more than 76 years.[41] If it hadn't been for lawyers, dedicated, hardworking lawyers, insistent on finding the truth, these six innocent people would still be in prison.

Say what you will about lawyers, but they actually do good in the world, more often than you might realize. Shakespeare had it wrong. Killing all the lawyers is not the solution to a legal profession gone off track. Changing what they do, and how they do it, can ensure that society benefits *because of* (not in *spite of*) them.

For me, the rewards of lawyering may not be so grand as to create groundbreaking legal precedent; they are simpler. I can close my eyes and in my mind see so many people that I have helped over the years, so many clients who have offered a heartfelt thank you for me standing next to them as they walked through some type of legal hell. I wrap a knit blanket around my shoulders, a gift from the sister of a criminal defendant client many years ago. I still remember the note that came with it. "Thank you for being like a warm blanket around our family during these difficult times."

About the author

M elody A. Kramer is an established innovator in the legal industry, a veteran trial lawyer, speaker, and author. Ms. Kramer is a graduate of the University of Nebraska, College of Law in Lincoln, Nebraska, and was awarded The Order of Barristers for excellence in the art of courtroom advocacy. Since that time, Ms. Kramer has been honing her craft as a vigorous advocate for her clients in federal, state, and tribal courts throughout the country.

Ms. Kramer began her career as a Deputy Public Defender in rural Nebraska, served as a Special Prosecutor for Crimes Against Children, and later started her own law firm in Lincoln, Nebraska. In 1999, she moved to California where she turned her focus to complex civil litigation, often in strategic partnership with other law firms. Never deterred by seeming impossibilities, she takes on challenging, sometimes seemingly unwinnable cases, with a marked level of success.

In addition to her legal practice, Ms. Kramer was actively involved with the Nebraska State Bar Association, including working on the Ethics Committee and the Judiciary Committee, the Sale of Law Practice Subcommittee, Gender/Bias Subcommittee, and the Bench/ Bar Conference Program Committees. Since moving to California, she turned her attention to broader issues facing the legal profession, including co-founding the National Association of Freelance Legal Professionals to raise visibility for the freelance segment of the legal profession and founding FreelanceLaw.com, an online resource for connecting law firms and freelance legal professionals. Most recently Ms. Kramer founded Legal Greenhouse, a think tank and developer of innovative legal solutions. In addition to this book, two key projects she will be focusing on are increased transparency in the judicial system, and research on the effects of the fight-or-flight response within the context of court proceedings.

Staying connected

If you enjoyed this book and want to get advance notice of the next book in the *Hacking the Legal System* series, join the mailing list at www.legalgreenhouse.com for advance notification.

If you are interested in having Ms. Kramer speak at an event, or to discuss collaboration opportunities, please contact her at the following:

Melody A. Kramer
4010 Sorrento Valley Blvd., Ste. 400
San Diego, CA 92121
melody@legalgreenhouse.com
www.legalgreenhouse.com
@legalgreenhouse.com

NOTES

1   Mehrabian, Albert. Silent Messages. Belmont, Calif.: Wadsworth
    Pub., 1971. Albert Mehrabian discusses his research on non-verbal
    communication. He concluded that prospects based their assessments of
    credibility on factors other than the words the salesperson spoke—the
    prospects studied assigned 55 percent of their weight to the speaker's
    body language and another 38 percent to the tone and music of their
    voice. They assigned only 7 percent of their credibility assessment to the
    salesperson's actual words.

2   Eaton, William W., James C. Anthony, Wallace Mandel, and Roberta
    Garrison. "Occupations and the Prevalence of Major Depressive Disorder."
    32 *Journal of Occupational and Environmental Medicine* (1990): 1079-087.

3   Randolph, K. "Why Lawyers Suck." Voter Vault Blog. November
    29, 2006. Accessed October 13, 2015. http://votervault.blogspot.
    com/2006/11/why-lawyers-suck.html

4   See "The LSAT." About the LSAT. Accessed October 13, 2015. http://
    www.lsac.org/jd/lsat/about-the-lsat.

5   Roscoe Pound was a former dean of both the University of Nebraska
    College of Law that I attended, and of Harvard Law School. Interestingly

related to this book, Pound was at one time a proponent of "legal realism," a school of thought that challenged prevailing thought that legal reasoning was separate and apart from moral and political discourse.

6   Nebraska Revised Statutes, 60-6,181

7   de Becker, Gavin. *The Gift of Fear: Survival Signals That Protect Us from Violence.* Boston: Little, Brown, 1997.

8   Turow, Scott. One L. New York: Putnam, 1977. 24-26. (emphasis added).

9   Turow, Scott. One L. New York: Putnam, 1977. 215.

10   Turow, Scott. One L. New York: Putnam, 1977. 264

11   See Kipp, Bill. Turning Fear into Power: The Fast Defense System. Boulder, Colo.: Paladin Press, 2005, for more history about the development of this program

12   Kipp, Bill. Turning Fear into Power: The Fast Defense System. Boulder, Colo.: Paladin Press, 2005.

13   See Muir, Ronda. "A Short History of the Billable Hour and the Consequences of Its Tyranny." Law People. June 18, 2007. Accessed

October 13, 2015. http://www.lawpeopleblog.com/2007/06/a-short-history-of-the-billable-hour-and-the-consequences-of-its-tyranny/.

14 A.B.A. Opinion 302 (November 27, 1961)

15 Goldfarb v. Virginia State Bar, 421 U.S. 773 (1975)

16 Kinsella, Sophie. The Undomestic Goddess. New York: Dial Press, 2005.

17 Cassens Weiss, Debra. "Did 'Financial Insanity' and 'Greedy Lawyers' Doom WolfBlock?" ABA Journal. May 14, 2009. Accessed October 13, 2015. http://www.abajournal.com/news/did_financial_insanity_and_greedy_lawyers_doom_wolfblock.

18 Mortazavi, Melissa. "Lawyers, Not Widgets: Why Private-Sector Attorneys Must Unionize to Save the Legal Profesion." Minnesota Law Review, April 1, 2012.

19 "An Early Look at The 2015 Am Law 100 Read More: Http://www.americanlawyer.com/id=1202717423172/An-Early-Look-at-The-2015-Am-Law-100-#ixzz3oTIpBDMO." The American Lawyer, 2015. http://www.americanlawyer.com/id=1202717423172/An-Early-Look-at-The-2015-Am-Law-100-.

20 Fried, Jason, and David Heinemeier Hansson. Rework. New York: Crown Business, 2010. pg. 25.

21 Fried, Jason, and David Heinemeier Hansson. Rework. New York: Crown Business, 2010. pg. 26.

22 Breitman, Rachel. "Stroock Defers Associates Too, Puts Forward Opt-Out Option." The AmLaw Daily. May 6, 2009. Accessed October 28, 2015. http://amlawdaily.typepad.com/amlawdaily/2009/05/stroock-makes-it-official-too.html.

23 Hill, Kashmir. "MoFo Sets Start Dates and Gives Out Stipends to Some." Above the Law. May 6, 2010. Accessed October 28, 2015. http://abovethelaw.com/2010/05/mofo-sets-start-dates-and-gives-out-stipends-to-some/.

24 Cassens Weiss, Debra. "Summer Associate Gripes: No BlackBerrys, Too Much Food and Booze." ABA Journal. October 9, 2008. Accessed October 28, 2015. http://www.abajournal.com/news/article/summer_associate_gripes_no_blackberrys_too_much_food_and_booze.

25 Lola v. Skadden, Arps, Slate, Meagher & Flom, United States District Court, Southern District of New York, Case No. 13-cv-5008 (RJS), Opinion and Order dated September 16, 2014. On July 23, 2015, however, the Second Circuit Court of Appeals vacated the dismissal and remanded the case (sent it back to the trial court level for further proceedings).

26 Frankel, Alison. "The Sad Tale of the Contract Lawyer Who Sued Skadden (and Lost)." September 17, 2014. Accessed October 13, 2015. http://blogs.reuters.com/alison-frankel/2014/09/17/the-sad-tale-of-the-contract-lawyer-who-sued-skadden-and-lost/.

27 Sedlik, Gary. "To Temp or Not to Temp." BCGSearch.com. February 10, 2009. Accessed October 13, 2015. http://www. lateralattorneyreport.com/2009/02/to-temp-or-not-to-temp/.

28 Miller, Joseph. "Jd Wired Fall 2007 Survey Results And Analysis." Jd Wired Fall 2007 Survey Results And Analysis. 2008. Accessed October 13, 2015. http://www.slideshare.net/JDWired/jd-wired-fall-2007-survey-results-and-analysis.

29 Jones, Ashby. "Newcomer Law Firms Are Creating Niches With Blue-Chip Clients." WSJ. July 2, 2008. Accessed October 28, 2015. http://www.wsj.com/article_email/SB121495897751221527-lMyQjAxMDI4MTA0MjkwNTI4Wj.html.

30 Jones, Ashby. "Newcomer Law Firms Are Creating Niches With Blue-Chip Clients." WSJ. July 2, 2008. Accessed November 2, 2015.

31 "Stay of Execution." Stay of Execution. Accessed Octoer 13, 2015. http://civpro.blogs.com/civil_procedure/2003/09/why_are_lawyers.html

32 Press, Aric, and John O'Connor. "Lessons of the Am Law 100 2008: The Big Firms Just Finished the Best Five-year Economic Run since We Began Keeping Records." The American Lawyer, 2008.

33 Kramer, Melody. "National Association of Freelance Legal Professionals." Quality vs. Quantity-The Billable Hour Mousetrap. January 28, 2009. Accessed October 13, 2015. http://freelancelegalprofessionals.blogspot.com/2009/01/quality-vs-quantity-billable-hour.html

34 www.acc.com

35 Before I proceed on with this sentence, let me say a word about the word "specialized" both to demonstrate what nut jobs lawyers have become and why I feel the necessity to make a disclaimer before I continue writing (as well as its impact on valuing lawyer services). Lawyers are prohibited from telling potential clients that they "specialize" in anything unless and until they become a "certified specialist" by their state bar association. It doesn't matter if you have practiced law for 30 years in the same niche practice, won accolades of clients, co-counsel, and judges alike, you cannot say you "specialize" in anything unless you have taken another test and paid another fee. And lest I forget, there is only a short list of available "specialties" so if you practice in another legal field, you can never describe yourself as a "specialist." I have yet to find any state that has available any "certified specialist" designations for litigation, so I guess I'm out of luck.

So, to clarify for the California State Bar or Nebraska State Bar Association, both of which I am a member, I am not using the term "specialize" for the purpose of describing my level of skill as a criminal defense attorney (I was a kickass criminal defense lawyer, by the way; just ask any of my former clients), but rather for the dictionary definition "to pursue a special activity, occupation, or field of study." I even co-authored two criminal prosecution manuals for the Nebraska County Attorney's Association, books that still sit on judge's bookshelves around the state. (By the way, to ensure that I don't get sued for copyright infringement, I must credit the source of that definition as being from www.thefreedictionary.com and I am not paying them any royalties for using this brief quote because I am invoking the fair use doctrine that exempts this use from constituting copyright infringement.)

36 *Miranda v. Arizona*, 384 U.S. 436 (1966)

174

37 Their criteria can be found here - US News and World Report Education. Accessed October 13, 2015. http://www.usnews.com/articles/education/best-graduate-schools/2008/03/26/law-methodology.html.

38 Page, Peter. "Change Ahead for Law School Rankings." The American Lawyer. July 7, 2008. Accessed November 2, 2015.

39 Kaplan, Ari. "A Revolution in Online Legal Content." Legal Tech Newsletter, July 7, 2008.

40 Hansen, Mark. "ABA Probes Lawyer Raters—Avvo, Am Law and Best Lawyers." ABA Journal. October 18, 2010. Accessed October 13, 2015. http://www.abajournal.com/news/article/aba_probes_lawyer_raters/

41 "Thomas Winslow Awarded $180,000 For 20 Years Imprisonment As 'Beatrice Six' Defendant." Justice Denied: The Journal for the Wrongfully Accused Spring 2011, no. 46. http://justicedenied.org/issue/issue_47/winslow_jd47.pdf.

Made in the USA
Las Vegas, NV
15 November 2020

10971228R00105